PSYCHIC POWERS

THE unXplained

PSYCHIC POWERS

SIMON TOMLIN

p

First published in 2000 by Parragon

Parragon
Queen Street House
4 Queen Street
Bath BA1 1HE, UK

Produced by Magpie Books, an imprint of
Constable Robinson Ltd, London

ISBN 0-75253-593-5

Illustrations courtesy of Fortean Picture Library

Page design by Sandie Boccacci

A copy of the British Library Cataloguing-in-Publication Data
is available from the British Library

Printed and bound in the EC

For my wife Dani, my inspiration in everything that I do.

With special thanks to Jonathan Clements – truly the best man.

Contents

●●

Contents •

THE MIND AND BEYOND

THE PSYCHICS

Introduction

• •

For as long as the human race has existed, certain individuals have been marked out by their societies as being "special". Some have been celebrated as exceptional athletes, powerful physically or with incredible endurance. Others have been marked out for their mental prowess in the fields of literature, mathematics, science – great thinkers who have revolutionized the way the rest of us view the world. Yet others have achieved fame and praise for their charitable efforts, devoting their lives to helping others less fortunate than themselves, often to their own personal detriment.

Societies should, and most usually do, praise these remarkable individuals. They have been singled out and lauded for their exceptional abilities and faith. Many, however, have been ridiculed and even punished for their talents. Galileo was suspected of heresy by the Spanish Inquisition, condemned to house arrest for life and forbidden to publish because of his beliefs. He believed that Copernicus's theory that the Earth revolved around the Sun was correct, a theory which all of us now take for granted as being the truth. Vincent van Gogh died a pauper and was considered mad. It was not until later that people began to appreciate his genius, and now his works of art are among the most celebrated in history. So has proven to be the case many, many times with those who have had extraordinary abilities which cannot be explained or understood by society in general. I refer, of course, to those with some form of psychic ability – a remarkable "gift" which marks them out as being special, though not for physical or mental prowess, but for something beyond any conventional wisdom, something bizarre, abnormal and unexplainable.

Religious leaders too have been followed and worshipped for centuries. Christians firmly believe that Jesus Christ was sent to Earth from another world (Heaven), with extraordinary abilities. He could perform miracles, including healing, which is recognized by many today as a form of psychic ability. Almost every religion has a similar figure who is believed to have possessed incredible powers of prophecy and healing – just think of Muhammed, Buddha, Krishna – the list goes on. Belief in, and worship of, these religious leaders obviously continues today but, in their time, many were considered by the masses to be a threat. They were unknown quantities, and any religious teaching will show that they suffered as a result. The Romans crucified Christ, and the sign of the cross is seen today as a celebration of his life by millions worldwide.

Others who have been seen as having remarkable powers have received differing treatments over the course of history. Psychic power, the paranormal and the belief that we are not alone in the universe have, throughout history, inspired, enthralled and, yes, terrified us. We have consistently responded according to the viewpoint of the masses, for better or worse. The ancient Greeks believed in the exceptional powers of the supernatural, and worshipped the oracle at Delphi, believing that they would be given an insight into the future, or given advice on the correct path to take in any given situation, by some divine power. In American Indian and African tribes, often the most powerful member of the tribe was the "medicine man" or "witch doctor". Both variants were believed to have the power to commune with the spirit world, and to travel at will into the "astral plane", the world of the collective unconscious. Shamanism still exists today, and medical science has been dumbfounded by the healing powers of the modern shaman.

However, as much as those with psychic powers have been celebrated in societies, they have been ridiculed, threatened, persecuted or even killed for their abilities. Fear is a powerful emotion, and fear of the unknown is something that we all suffer from. Throughout the centuries, this has led to the deaths of many who were believed to have "supernatural" powers. Witch-hunts were performed throughout the world for centuries in the belief that supernatural powers were the work of the devil, and poor unfortunate souls were possessed by demons. The only way to rid a soul of the devil was to kill, usually by fire, the person who was possessed.

The most famous example of this happened in America as late as 1692. The events which led to the Salem Witch Trials occurred in what is now the town of Danvers, then a parish of Salem Town, known as Salem Village. What launched the hysteria was the inexplicable behaviour of two young girls; nine-year-old Elizabeth Parris and eleven-year-old Abigail Williams. Elizabeth Parris was the daughter of the Salem Village minister, and Abigail Williams his niece. Both girls began to exhibit strange behaviour, including blasphemous screaming, trance-like states and convulsive seizures. Within a short time, several other girls in the village began to show signs of similar behaviour. Local physicians were unable to explain any physical cause for the symptoms, and concluded that the girls were under the influence of demonic possession. The girls were pressed to identify the source of their curse, and they named three women – Sarah Good, Sarah Osbourne and Tituba, Reverend Parris's Caribbean Indian slave.

Sarah Good and Sarah Osbourne both pleaded their innocence, but Tituba testified to seeing the devil, whom she claimed appeared to her "sometimes like a hog and sometimes like a great dog". More damning than that, Tituba confessed that there was a conspiracy of witches working in Salem. Over the following weeks, other villagers came forward and confessed that they had seen or been harmed by strange phenomena caused by some of the community members. Accusations flew wildly around, and the most frequently accused were women whose behaviour or financial situations were somehow disturbing to the social order and conventions of the time. Many people confessed to witchcraft, but only under great duress. One such was Margaret Jacobs, who at her trial told the court:

> *"They told me if I would not confess I should be put down into the dungeon and would be hanged, but if I would confess I should save my life."*

By the time the hysteria died down, twenty-four people had died as a direct result of the witch trials.

Nineteen were executed by hanging, but some died in prison. Giles Corey maintained his innocence after he had been accused of witchcraft, and later refused to stand trial. His refusal meant that he could not legally be convicted, but such was the prevailing brutality and hysteria in the town, that he was "interrogated" by placing stone weights on his body. He spent two days undergoing this barbaric torture before he died.

Unexplained phenomena are as commonplace today as they ever have been. The current view, however, is far removed from the Salem Witch Trials of 300 years ago. Modern societies are just as baffled by some of the amazing things that go on in the world, but we are less fearful of psychic powers and the supernatural. In fact, if we are honest, most of us are fascinated, awed by such events. Interest in the supernatural and the paranormal has never been so strong in the Western world as it is today.

Many people dedicate their lives to the study of psychic powers, in one form or another. On the one side are the parapsychologists, who seek to find explanations for phenomena which are beyond current human comprehension. Societies to investigate these phenomena operate throughout the world, and many leading scientists devote their intellectual abilities to the research programmes. In the opposing camp are the debunkers who seek to detect psychic hoaxes, and use this evidence to refute the claims of all alleged psychics. One man has dedicated his life to exposing the whole area of the supernatural and paranormal as a confidence trick. We shall see the views of this man, James Randi, throughout this book, in contrast to the many amazing claims of the psychics themselves.

In general, though, the West has become far more

tolerant of the claims of psychics. More tolerant, and more interested. Science has progressed in leaps and bounds over the last two centuries, at the expense of research into the mind and its powers. As Nikola Tesla, a great Russian physicist and mystic once said,

> *"On that day when science begins to investigate non-physical phenomena, it will make greater progress in a decade than in all the centuries it has existed."*

Science has made a start. The research into psychic powers is under way. But I think that it will take considerably more than a decade to uncover the secrets of the human mind.

Before Science

●●●●●●●●●●●●●●●●●●●●●●●●●●●●●●●●●●●●●●

Paranormal and supernatural

The terms "paranormal" and "supernatural" are relatively recent additions to the language. "Paranormal" literally means "abnormal; not susceptible to normal explanations", and "supernatural" means "above or beyond nature". The reason that they are new words is because advances in scientific study over the last 500 years have led to a greater understanding of the world around us. Prior to this, paranormal and supernatural did not exist in the minds of the general population. "Para" and "super" were, quite simply, normal. Anything which could not be explained according to the five senses was either the work of the gods, or something generated by a sixth sense which a few talented people had.

It was not only the growth of the scientific movement which stifled belief in psychic powers; the spread of Christianity, in particular Roman Catholicism, soon changed the way people felt. The strict doctrines of the religious leaders led Western civilizations to explain away anyone with extraordinary abilities as a heretic if they were lucky, or a witch if they were not. Throughout the last millennium, thousands of people were slaughtered for having beliefs which were not 100 per cent in line with the

Roman Catholic church. The civilized world in earlier centuries was by modern standards a savage, brutal and terrifying place. The apex of this horror, and perse-cution of anyone seen to have offended against religious laws, came with the Holy Inquisition, which first came into existence in 1231. A succession of papal commands increased the powers of the Inquisition, until it reached its most terrifying aspect with the appointment of Tomás de Torquemada as the Inquisitor-General of the Spanish arm of the Inquisition in 1483. The Spanish Inquisition itself claimed 309,000 victims, most of whom were burned to death for their religious views, or for "witchcraft".

It is small wonder that it has taken centuries for the West to re-enter a discussion on psychic phenomena. Even as late as 1917, the Roman Catholic church denounced certain psychic abilities as heresy. That, coupled with the incredible achievements of the scien-tific community, has meant that even intellectuals who research into psi phenomena (paranormal or psychic phenomena collectively) are often regarded as cranks. But then, so were Einstein, Copernicus, Van Gogh and Charles Darwin. The interest in psychic ability prior to the Victorian age was confined to one aspect only. Any phenomenon which could not be explained was either ignored or classed as a miracle in the eyes of God. Great healers, who could lay on hands, were revered as saints; for this was the only way to celebrate them without fear of reprisal from the church. Nowadays, they would be studied as mystics, psychics with excep-tional abilities, but it is very doubtful that they would be canonized for their skills.

The interest in Spiritualism and psi started in the middle of the nineteenth century. Perhaps this was a backlash against the increasing industrialization of the world. It is equally possible that, as our understanding of the world around us became ever greater, we actively sought phenomena that science could not explain. Over 150 years later, many of those phenomena have been explained, or cast aside as fraudulent. Many, however, have not. Science is slowly coming round to the idea that research should be conducted into psychic power, especially in the light of mounting evidence that it exists. The Western world has grown increasingly reliant on science to explain everything, but deep down in us all there is a part that won't let go of our ancestral beliefs in the paranormal. What it essentially boils down to is a fear that once we have lived our lives on this planet, there is nothing to come afterwards. Both science and parapsychology seek to find answers to the eternal question: what happens to us when we die?

Certain psychic abilities appear to confirm the existence of an afterlife. Spirit summonings, communing with the dead, stories of reincarnation, receiving messages from the spirit world through clairaudience and clairvoyance and out-of-the-body experiences, all point to the same thing. Either there is life after death, a spirit world or a collective unconscious from which a special few can draw inspiration. At the turn of a new millennium, the world is still waiting for the answers. What remains to be seen is who will come up with them first: the scientists, the psychologists or the researchers into parapsychology and the powers of the mind?

Spirit Summonings

• •

Where do we go from here?

Humankind has always been obsessed by the question "What happens to us after death?", and understandably so. All ancient and modern religions address the question, indeed for most religions, the whole purpose of life as we know it on Earth is as a means of passage into the next world. This then leads on to the question of what part of us continues to exist beyond the death of the body, or "what leaves a living body to render it dead"?

The Chinese call this "qi" (pronounced chee); the ancient Egyptians referred to it as "ka"; and the ancient Greeks considered it to be the "psyche". All three, if pronounced correctly, are very "breathy" words. This is because it was believed that the last thing to leave a living body was the breath, and this therefore must be the soul or spirit. Once the last breath has left a body, the body is dead, but the breath floats away and still exists. It was, and still is, a common belief that the spirit moves on to another plane. This, to Christians, is either heaven or hell, and takes similar forms in most modern religions. At its most basic, this plane is inhabited by many spirits and, in one form or another, spirit gods. To Christians, these are represented by angels, saints and God himself. In times of great strife, people have often attempted to contact the spirit world for help, advice or healing.

Spirit Gods

The concept of the spirit is one that most people would agree with, in one shape or form. Many religions believe in and actively worship spirit gods. Such spirit gods are believed to control certain facets of the world around us. One god may represent food, another will personify fire, another characterizes love, and another war. Followers of these gods believe that the spirits can help them, and can be called upon through sacrifices and worship.

Nearly 500 years ago, tribesmen from villages in West Africa were transported to Brazil, to be sold as slaves. When they arrived, after an horrific journey across seas of which they had no knowledge, they immediately offered thanks to their goddess of the sea, and mother of all spirits, Iemanja. They erected altars to honour her, for they firmly believed that it was she, their Spirit God, who had ensured their safe passage across the sea.

At the time, the Roman Catholic church was intolerant of anyone worshipping what they deemed to be "false gods", and attempted to impose Catholic beliefs upon the tribesmen. Despite all their efforts, they were only in part successful. The tribesmen were all too willing to worship images of the Virgin Mary and Jesus Christ, but the image of the Virgin Mary to them would always be their mother spirit Iemanja. They worshipped Christ as Oxalus, the god of purity and goodness, and Xango, the spirit of the wilderness, was synonymous with John the Baptist. Every year in Brazil, New Year's Eve celebrations are still held in honour of Iemanja, the goddess who protected the slaves on their perilous journey 500 years ago.

Many spiritual or religious "cults" claim that they can summon up their Spirit Gods. Devotees claim that major religions are too remote from their own gods to be able to summon them, and only intimate contact with these Spirit Gods enables them to be summoned. One much maligned and misunderstood example of such a spiritual belief system is the voodoo cult of Haiti.

Voodoo is generally associated with the "dark side" of psychic power. When most people are asked what the word "voodoo" means to them, they will think of witchcraft, black magic and curses. Images of ritual slaughter of animals and wild, frenzied dancing appear in the mind. However, devotees of voodoo believe in the summoning of a Spirit God who is believed to have the power to heal those who come to him. This Spirit God is commonly referred to as the "Old Black Slave". (Other Spirit Gods of the voodoo are called upon to bring luck, money or love, or to ward off evil forces.) It is true that invoking the Spirit God usually involves rituals, more often than not in the form of frenzied dancing. These wild gyrations continue until the receptor of the Spirit God becomes "possessed" by his spirit, and thereby empowered with the ability to heal. Voodoo priests and priestesses have described themselves as being "ridden by divine horsemen", and fully believe that in this trance-like state, they are as one with the Old Black Slave.

Modern psychologists are very dismissive of such

beliefs. Rather, they claim that the person who is seemingly possessed by the spirit god, is in fact experiencing what is termed "dissociation of consciousness". By subjecting themselves to such single-minded and frenzied behaviour prior to the "possession", the individual has suppressed into the unconscious all parts of the mind save for one segment, which takes control over the entire mind, and forces the body into strange and uncharacteristic behaviour. In many ways, this is a very convincing theory. The repetitive nature of the dancing, the chanting, the drums and the belief in the likely outcome could well trigger the mind to believe that it was actually possessed by spirits. One of the voodoo gods is an Earth-force depicted as a snake-god called *Damballah*. Sure enough, those worshippers of Damballah who become possessed by his spirit never speak, but only hiss, and will often wriggle along the ground or climb trees. Perhaps the psychologists are right, and the whole concept of voodoo can be neatly categorized under the aforementioned label "dissociation of consciousness".

But what of those individuals who have benefited from the healing powers of the Old Black Slave? Psychologists, doctors and surgeons have been unable to refute the power of alternative medicine completely, and have only come up with one explanation for the healing powers of voodoo priests and priestesses. The theory is that the healing process is psychosomatic – the individual's faith in the healing power of the "possessed" priest or priestess is so strong that they *believe* that they will be healed of their ailment. The mind interfaces with the body, and the healing process speeds up due to the force of will of the afflicted individual. This argument holds more sway than one of

Guide to the major voodoo Spirit Gods

Name	Symbol	Has power over	Sacrifice	Sacred colour	Signs of possession
Ogou	A sabre half buried in the ground	Blacksmiths, fire and war	Rams, bulls, red cockerels	Red	
Damballah	A rainbow of snakes	Luck, journeys, wealth, happiness	A pair of white chickens, rice, milk and eggs	White	Writhing on the ground like a snake
Ayida	Two snakes with three stars between them	Good luck at initiation ceremonies	Eggs, milk and rice	Rainbow colours	Wriggling on the ground like a snake
Agwe	Star with plumes	The sea, boats and sailors	Goats, peppers, champagne and fine wine	White, green and pink	Being drawn to water, diving and swimming

15

mere coincidence, but we have returned to the power of the mind over the body. Is psychosomatic healing as much a psychic power as summoning up a Spirit God?

The fact remains that belief is a powerful force. Whether beliefs have a scientific grounding or not surely doesn't matter. If a voodoo follower truly believes that he or she has summoned a Spirit God, and the result is that he or she cures another individual, then so be it.

Séances

The ability to summon spirits is no longer solely a power possessed by tribal communities. Ever since the birth of the Spiritualist movement (see Chapter 6) in the nineteenth century, Western societies have become much more interested in exploring psychic powers. During Victorian times, holding a séance was very fashionable; many mediums in the latter half of the nineteenth century became rich and famous for their ability to summon up spirits in Victorian parlours, and were even consulted by Queen Victoria herself. Perhaps the most famous of them all was a very controversial figure, Daniel Dunglas Home.

In 1855, Home became the houseguest of a famous London solicitor, John Rymer, and his wife. They were more than happy for the famous medium to stay with them, as they believed that he had put them in touch with the spirit of their dead child, and Home's séances at their house became the talk of London. One of Home's most famous summonings happened on 23 July 1855. It became a famous event because of the people Home had invited to attend – the celebrated

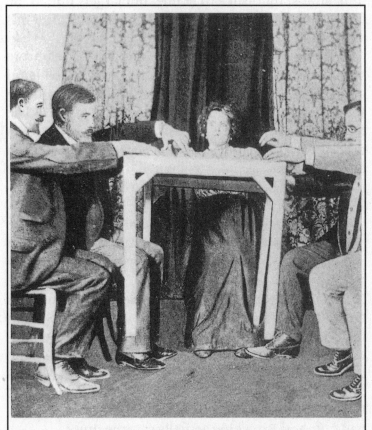

A medium in a trance, talking with the other side.

poets, Robert Browning and Elizabeth Barrett Browning. On arrival at the house, Robert Browning took an instant dislike to Home, but largely due to the interest displayed by his wife, he remained courteous to the medium.

At 9 p.m., the séance began. Fourteen people were seated around a cloth-covered table, with an oil lamp at its centre. Home fell into a trance, and soon those seated around the table heard rapping noises. The table then began tilting and vibrating of its own accord. Suddenly it reared up at a steep angle, but the lamp remained in place as though it were glued to the table; Robert Browning said of it afterwards,

> "... all hands were visible. I don't know at all how the thing was done ... all the raps seemed from or about the table, not the region outside us."

This could very easily have been explained away as an elaborate fraud, but the séance progressed to include much more physical phenomena. The Rymers, who were present at the séance, both felt something touch them, and stated that they believed that it was the spirit of their dead son, Wat. Elizabeth Barrett Browning then felt her dress being lifted by an unseen hand. Robert Browning actually saw the dress

> "uplifted in a manner I cannot account for – as if by some object inside – which could hardly have been introduced there without her becoming aware of it."

The oil lamp was then, at the "request" of the spirit, extinguished. In the half-light of the room, the guests saw a ghostly hand appear at the edge of the table, opposite the Brownings. More hands appeared, and one picked up a small bell from the table and rang it. Robert Browning was very sceptical about the appearance of the hands, and reported that they always remained close to Home, never moving into the open space of the room. Through a series of rapping noises, the spirit communicated that Robert Browning would be allowed to touch one of the hands, but when he pressed the point, he was told that he could not after all.

Elizabeth Barrett Browning, however, was convinced of the validity of the proceedings, and while the room was still in darkness, Home asked her to sit next to him. The ghostly hands then took a flowery wreath from the table and placed it upon her head. Neither she nor her husband could explain how that happened. The guests were then asked to leave the room for fifteen minutes, and when they were called back in, the lights had been lit once more. Home announced that the spirits would now lift the table off the floor, so that Robert Browning could examine the phenomenon and put his scepticism to rest.

Browning wrote of the events:

> *"I looked under the table, and can aver that it was lifted from the ground, say a foot high, more than once – Mr Home's hands being plainly above it."*

The séance then ended. Browning reported that he could not explain how the events had happened, but he still remained deeply sceptical of Home's abilities. He even wrote a poem, "Mr Sludge, the Medium", which satirized what he believed to be the fraudulent work of the mediums.

Home had many detractors who claimed he was a fraud; among them were Charles Dickens and Harry Houdini. Dickens denounced him as "a ruffian and a scoundrel", and Houdini announced that he could repeat any of Home's phenomena himself by trickery. Home's work is still the subject of controversy, and there is still speculation over whether he was a genuine medium, or a fraud. Many thought that his greatness lay not with what he did, but with what the people who saw him at work *thought* he did. Not once, however, was Home ever proven to have committed a fraud, not in twenty years of mediumship.

When Home died of tuberculosis in 1886, he left quite a gap. He had become the most celebrated medium of his time, performing countless séances, and convincing thousands of people of the existence of the spirit world. In 1874 that gap was filled by a young woman named Florence Cook, who went much further than Home. She was able to summon not only ghostly rappings and moving tables, but also very real apparitions of the spirits themselves. Hard, tangible evidence of the spirit world to some; a perverse, elaborate hoax to others.

By the time Florence Cook became a medium, it had become the fashion to bind mediums as prevention against fraud. In 1874, securely bound, Florence Cook fell into a trance during one of her most famous séances. The curtains behind her moved, and then parted, to reveal the ghostly figure of a woman. To the amazement of the people in the room, the figure came out from the curtains and further materialized, taking on a much stronger physical presence. The spirit announced that she was the ghost of Katie King, the long-dead daughter of a pirate; Florence had summoned her from the spirit world, and she had come.

The ghost circulated the room, speaking with and touching the guests at the séance table. She even posed for photographs before she disappeared. Was this ghostly materialization what humankind had yearned for for centuries – undeniable proof of the existence of the afterlife? Or was it an elaborate hoax? One of the members of the audience was William Crookes, one of the most brilliant scientists of the time and a pioneer in the fields of chemistry and physics. If anyone would denounce the appearance of Katie King's ghost as a fraud, it would surely be him. But Crookes, the cool rational scientist, could not explain what he had seen, and rather than denounce the séance, he instead came to champion Florence Cook's extraordinary powers as a psychic and medium.

If ever there is a champion of a person's psychic abilities, there will be a hundred sceptics who wish to disprove them. Crookes may have offered his support to Florence Cook, but there were many others who wished to disprove her abilities. Many such people had pointed out that the apparition of Katie King bore a quite striking resemblance to Florence herself, and although the ghost would readily pose for photographs, there had never been any photographs of Florence and Katie together.

Florence was gaining great fame as a spirit summoner until, during one of her sittings, someone grabbed the apparition – a serious breach of séance etiquette at the time. It was believed that the spirit took its form from essences of the medium's body, and touching the spirit could harm or even kill the medium. During one of Florence's séances, however,

William Volckman committed such an act. He grabbed hold of the spirit and refused to let go until, with the aid of some of the other participants, the "spirit" managed to free itself.

Florence was at the time in a "medium's cabinet", hidden by curtains. When the apparition went away, those present opened the curtains to find Florence still bound up, but looking dishevelled. William Volckman declared to all those present that the spirit of Katie King was in fact Florence Cook wearing white drapery. Florence protested her innocence, and to prove that she was not a fraud, she offered to subject herself to strict scientific testing. Who better to perform those tests than the now confirmed believer in spiritualism, William Crookes? Florence offered herself to Crookes for testing, and he was only too keen to oblige, wishing to remove the slur on her good reputation.

The two of them undertook a series of séances that lasted for five months. For Crookes, the test of Florence's authenticity was simple: all she had to do was to prove to him that Katie King and Florence Cook could be seen by him at the same time, thus proving that the medium and the spirit were not the same person. At the end of the series of séances, Crookes alleged that he had indeed seen the medium and the spirit together on two separate occasions. He also claimed to have photographed Katie and Florence together, but their faces were never visible at the same time in the photographs. Florence had had to cover her face because she was sensitive to the strong light that the camera required. Crookes also noted essential differences between Katie and Florence. Katie was taller than Florence and had long blond hair, whereas Florence's hair was short and dark. Crookes never, however, considered the possibility that Florence might have had an accomplice.

Crookes studied the paranormal for five years before an event caused him to abandon his psychical research. Another medium, Mary Showers, confessed to him that her séances were complete frauds. Mary and Florence were great friends and had often performed joint sittings for Crookes in the past. He could not possibly believe that one of them was a fraud and the other genuine, although he never denounced Florence as a fraud, nor did he even renounce his endorsement of her as a true psychic.

The substance of the spirits

Whether Florence was capable of summoning spirits, or just a clever fraudster, we will never know for sure. Many other psychics claimed the ability to produce apparitions during séances for years to come, until a new phenomenon started to appear – ectoplasm.

One of the most controversial mediums of the late nineteenth and early twentieth centuries was a southern Italian lady called Eusapia Palladino. Palladino broke the mould: where most mediums of the Victorian age were young, attractive females, Palladino was short, dumpy and unkempt. She was a coarse, country girl who was illiterate, but she managed time and time again to stun leading aristocrats with her incredible abilities. Palladino is one of the most vigorously tested mediums in history, and the results are still argued over today. She was known to cheat – she even admitted to it several times, but on many other occasions she asserted that she was

The substance of the spirits?

genuine, and these remarkable sittings were under constant supervision.

On one occasion, Palladino performed a séance in front of the Milan Commission. They were so amazed by her abilities that they endorsed her psychic ability as genuine, with only one dissenter among them. That dissenter was Dr Charles Richet of France, a very well-respected professor of physiology who later won a Nobel prize. He did not believe that Palladino was genuinely able to contact the spirit world, and so he invited her to an island he owned off the south coast of France. He also invited two leading members of the Society for Psychical Research and several other "psychic investigators", all of whom had had much experience investigating séances.

Richet arranged for Palladino to perform a séance under strict controls. During the séance, one of the investigators held Palladino's right hand, another her left hand, with an observer under the table holding her feet. The lights in the room were kept on so that no trickery could take place under cover of darkness. Palladino managed, under these conditions, to raise a large melon and a wicker table from behind her on to the séance table. Even the most hardened of the sceptics present in the room concluded that some of the phenomena they had witnessed were supernatural.

The group decided to perform further observations on Palladino, and this time they made it very easy for her to commit a fraud. She duly obliged, and was, according to the Society for Psychical Research, officially debunked. But her career continued to thrive despite this, and she was successfully tested by Marie and Pierre Curie among others. The Society for Psychical Research could not ignore her, and decided to re-test her abilities, using Everard Fielding, a self-confessed sceptic who had a long record of debunking frauds.

Fielding made extensive notes on eleven séances Palladino held under his strict observation. He described her impressive psychokinetic abilities, and a most strange phenomenon, the like of which he had never before seen. Palladino seemed to grow new limbs from her body, some sort of pseudopodia which Fielding described as "curious long black knobbly things with cauliflowers at the end of them". Ectoplasm had arrived on the scene.

Palladino may have been the first on record to produce ectoplasm – the substance of the spirits – but its master was another psychic medium who took the name "Eva C". In 1905 Charles Richet, the famous scientist and paranormal investigator, was called to a French military installation in Algiers to study a medium called Marthe Béraud. Marthe was living with a French general and his wife, the Noels, and was supposedly able to summon the spirit of an Indian Brahman known as Bien Boa.

Richet discovered that Marthe was able to produce, in his words,

> *"a kind of liquid paste or jelly that emerges from the mouth or the breast of Marthe, which organizes itself by degrees, acquiring the shape of a face or a limb."*

The spirit of Bien Boa apparently formed itself in ectoplasm from Marthe's body. Richet took numerous photographs of the "spirit" and proved that it was not Marthe in disguise – the two of them could be seen together. Bien Boa would usually appear while the curtains of the medium's cabinet were closed, and then wander among the guests while the curtains were open, and Marthe could be seen in a trance. Richet undertook a thorough examination of the séance room, and reported that nothing could enter the room or the cabinet without being seen by the audience. Shortly afterwards, however, Marthe was heavily implicated in a fraud and moved to Paris, changing her name to Eva Carriére, or Eva C.

Eva C's fame grew steadily as tales of her ecto-plasmic emissions became more widespread. She came to the attention of another famous scientist, Schrenck-Notzing, who began investigating her in 1909. He discovered that Eva was able to produce all manner of emissions from her body, most often from her mouth.

By 1911, Eva's ectoplasmic emissions had taken on definite form. She was able to produce whole limbs, followed by faces, which usually appeared on the back of her head. These faces, however, appeared very two-dimensional, and never moved. On one occasion, a sceptic in the audience noticed that one of these "ghostly" faces bore the words "Le Miro". The phantom head had appeared in a publication, *Le Miroir*, so was this ectoplasm simply a photograph cut from a magazine? Schrenck-Notzing thought not. He believed that Eva had a condition called hypermnesia, a very powerful memory. Eva was not producing spirits, but was producing images from her own body. The ectoplasm was real enough, but was not a ghost, it was an image from Eva's memory.

No one was able to explain how the ectoplasm was formed, until Eva came under investigation by the

Society for Psychical Research in 1920. They managed to obtain a sample of her ectoplasm and analyse it. It turned out to be chewed-up paper, prompting the society to announce that her ectoplasm was somehow regurgitated during her séances. Eva C disappeared from the scene soon afterwards.

The phenomenon of mediums able to produce ectoplasm has, like so many areas of psychic powers, never been proven or disproven. Its appearances seem to have been limited to the late nineteenth and early twentieth centuries – reports of it no longer come in. Many believe that the phenomenon was never really disproved because of the willingness of observers to believe in its existence. James Randi, the most famous debunker of them all, notes that observers at séances during the time were warned against touching the substance for fear that it may harm them. Randi added, "It may be that the reputation of the medium might also suffer."

A modern witch-hunt: the case of Helen Duncan

Helen Duncan is viewed by many spiritualists and psychics as a modern martyr, who suffered unnecessarily at the hands of a paranoid establishment which regarded her psychic abilities with deep scorn.

Helen Duncan was born in the central belt of Scotland to a poor family, and supplemented her income from the local bleach factory by performing spiritual work in the evenings. During the 1930s and 1940s, Helen travelled the length and breadth of Britain to hold séances in people's homes and in

Spiritualist churches. A gentleman called Vincent Woodcock was present at one of her sittings with his sister-in-law, and what he saw changed his life. Helen slipped into a trance and began to issue the by now much-maligned ectoplasm. Before his very eyes, the ectoplasm took on the form of his dead wife, who then asked both Vincent and his sister-in-law to stand up. The spirit then removed her own wedding ring, placed it on her sister's hand and said, "It is my wish that this takes place for the sake of my little girl." Within a year, Vincent married his former sister-in-law.

Helen was in great demand during World War II with relatives of those who had gone to fight. She was holding a séance in Portsmouth on 19 January 1944, when the meeting was interrupted by one of the guests blowing a whistle. The gentleman in question was a plain-clothes policeman, and his whistle signalled the beginning of a raid. Helen Duncan was arrested and charged with, of all things, vagrancy. Helen was refused bail, even though the maximum fine for vagrancy was a mere five shillings. She was sent to London, where she spent four days in the notorious women's prison, Holloway. While she was in there, the authorities debated her charge, and it was changed from one of vagrancy to one of conspiracy. During the war years, the penalty for conspiracy was death by hanging.

Her case was referred to the Old Bailey, the central criminal court, and the charges against her were changed yet again. Now she was accused of witchcraft, under an archaic statute dating back to 1735, just forty-three years after the horrors of the Salem Witch Trials in America. Helen was further accused under the Larceny Act of taking money "by falsely pretending she was in a position to bring about the appearances of these spirits of deceased persons".

Her trial lasted for seven days, and proved to be one of the biggest media spectacles at the time, attracting front-page headlines despite the fact that Britain was at war. Witnesses were brought in from all over the world to testify to Helen's abilities. Vincent Woodcock gave testimony to the events which led to his second marriage, as detailed above. Alfred Dodd, a highly respected academic and author, gave an account of a sitting that he had attended at Helen's home. His deceased grandfather had materialized in front of him, and had turned to Alfred's friend Tom, imploring him to look at his face, and then to compare it with a portrait which Alfred had of his own grandfather. Tom did so, and they found that the two were identical. James Herries, a journalist of some repute and a Justice of the Peace, took the stand. He testified that at one of Helen Duncan's séances, he had seen the spirit of Sir Arthur Conan Doyle materialize, and was convinced that it was not a fraud.

Helen Duncan's defence lawyers then decided to pursue a different tack. The prosecution was obsessed with proving her a fraud, so the defence asked that she be permitted to show her psychic skills in the courtroom. The prosecution alleged that such a display would ridicule the English legal system, and permission was refused. The jury took only half an hour to find her guilty of conspiracy to contravene the 1735 Witchcraft Act, but not guilty on all other charges.

In summary, the Portsmouth chief of police then

added further details for the judge to consider before sentencing. He alleged that in 1941 Helen Duncan had described the sinking of one of the Royal Navy's ships, the *Barham*, three months before the event had been made public. How could she have known that this would happen, unless she was a conspirator? The judge sentenced Helen to nine months' imprisonment in Holloway. The Spiritualist movement in Britain was incensed by the decision, and demanded a change in the law. They firmly believed that she had been imprisoned to prevent any wartime security leaks, and not for any fraud. The case went to appeal at the House of Lords, where again the defendant lost and her sentence was upheld, despite some of the greatest legal minds of the time denouncing the case as a miscarriage of justice. Winston Churchill even intervened at one point, declaring the whole situation a farce and a waste of both time and money. Even he, however, could not overturn the decision, and Helen served her nine months in Holloway.

In 1951, the 1735 Witchcraft Act was finally repealed and replaced with the Fraudulent Mediums Act. Three years later, Spiritualism was granted status as an official religion by a formal Act of Parliament. It seemed that the authorities wished to prevent any more witch-hunts.

In 1956, however, the police raided a séance taking place in Nottingham. They seized the medium while she was in a trance, something which should never be done because it can cause terrible damage. That medium was Helen Duncan and, as a result of the assault, she suffered burns to the stomach. Five weeks later she was dead.

Cosmic Connections

●●●●●●●●●●●●●●●●●●●●●●●●●●●●●●●

Angelic visits

Angels are probably the best known of all supernatural entities, with perhaps the exception of ghosts. Most mythological and religious philosophies embrace the concept of angels, seeing them as beings inhabiting the afterlife and, unlike most of the dead, enjoying certain privileges such as being able to visit the earth and take on visible forms.

The view that angels may reflect some kind of "other" reality has gained more strength during the 1990s, thanks to an apparent epidemic of angelic visions. These visions are usually one-off experiences in which individuals claim to have been rescued from life-threatening situations by some form of "guardian angel". These reports have existed for centuries, but the idea that supernatural help can directly impinge upon someone's life is more prevalent today than for several centuries.

Many view the appearance of an angel in a person's life as a form of voluntary possession, whereby the person affected allows a spirit to channel itself through them in order to escape an impossible situation. The sceptical interpretation of an angel is that it is a form of hallucination created from within the mind in a

Messengers from God, or figments of the imagination?

moment of crisis, and not a real entity. Researchers into the phenomenon disagree with this opinion – after all, how could an invention of the mind, which sceptics say is there to ease someone through a traumatic moment, actually help to save a person's life?

The research into angelic visions is a relatively new field, and is mainly restricted to religious organizations. This makes sense, as religions have a vested interest in proving the existence of angels, but some serious scientific investigation is also under way.

There are several famous cases of angelic intervention. One such case involved a lady by the name of Jessica Bellman from Los Angeles (the city of Angels!). Jessica was driving with her mother on a freeway near Hollywood during fast, bumper-to-bumper rush-hour traffic. Suddenly, ahead of them a large truck lost control and jack-knifed across the freeway. Jessica slammed on her brakes, sending her car into a spin and causing it to move sideways into three lanes of fast-moving traffic. Then the "miracle" as Bellman saw it, happened. Time seemed to slow down and the world became silent. Jessica recalls praying for help, and seeing her mother's eyes wide with terror. She remembers seeing a smiling, blond-haired, white-skinned entity, guiding her car through the carnage to safety. Jessica fully believes that she was in the presence of an angel, and that this entity had saved her life and the life of her mother.

A very strange series of happenings occurred at the Copper Ridge Baptist church near Knoxville, Tennessee. Parishioners reported seeing crosses of golden light on the church window, starting in November 1995. The minister, Reverend Bullard, was one of a small group of people who also saw glowing figures inside the church. These cloudy forms included a man in a turban and two other men in suits. All were fully formed, very clear and moved towards the wall of the church. One of them even turned and waved to the awe-struck onlookers. Once they reached the wall, they all disappeared.

A photographer managed to take some excellent shots of the phenomena. She reported that the crosses only appeared when there was a light source such as bright sunlight shining through the window. This was thought to provide an explanation – the appearance of the crosses was simply light refracting through the window – even though the crosses appeared to float in the air just outside the church, taking on the appearance of holograms. The theory of light refraction was taken seriously by the authorities, and they decided to replace the windows, but the crosses continued to appear.

Some of the local people claimed to have seen angels within the golden glow of the crosses. One of the townspeople said that if you walked towards the angel it vanished, just as you were about to touch it. Sceptics said that this indicated that the cross was being transformed into some form of illusion by the vivid imagination of the local people. A very possible explanation, but it does not explain the "miracle healings" that began to take place shortly after the appearance of the crosses and the "angels".

Two deaf children who lived in the town were out shopping with their mother. When they went into the greengrocer's, they claimed to have spoken with an angel, whom they described as "a tall man wearing a nice, light suit and a wonderful smile". Apparently he communicated with the deaf children using telepathy, and advised them to seek a cure for their deafness at the church. The Reverend Bullard invited the family to view the mysterious crosses, and one of the children communicated through sign language that she had seen Jesus walk out of the glowing crucifix. Within two weeks, both children's hearing was partially restored, and the medical community had no explanation for how that could have happened.

A very recent case of contact with "angels" involved a NASA space shuttle in February 1997. The *Discovery* was attempting a repair mission on the Hubble telescope when two crew members returning from a space walk observed a brightly coloured light passing the front of the shuttle, as though guiding them to safety. The event was being recorded on radio satellite transmissions sent back to Earth, but NASA scientists at Houston turned the transmissions off to prevent amateur space watchers picking up the sounds and pictures. However, one amateur managed to record the encounter on audio tape until he saw a technician walk across and flip a switch which ended the transmission.

The flight log for the *Discovery* revealed a twenty-minute gap in the official tapes, but NASA issued a statement claiming that there was nothing supernatural about the recorded conversation of the astronauts. Despite the awe in their voices, the official line was that they were merely tired, and that they must have mistaken a warning light on the console for something spectral outside their window. Whatever the real story was, the next spacewalk was cancelled and the *Discovery* returned immediately to Earth.

There are many theories which set out to explain the

appearance of angels. Naturally, those with strong religious beliefs are eager simply to regard them as messengers from God, sent to help out those in great peril on Earth. Some parapsychologists regard them as a form of voluntary possession, where spirits claiming to be angels are channelled through mediums and actually take on physical form. Others would explain that they are simply a figment of the imagination. But there is one other theory, which is an expansion of the channelling theory. Could it be that angels are not messengers from God, but messengers from another planet?

New age channellers

For centuries, mediums have claimed to be able to channel messages from the other side, from the spirits of the dead. A relatively new phenomenon, however, known as channelling, has started to manifest itself in the last fifty years or so. There has been a huge increase in the number of people who claim to have received information from some other realm, information which seeks to guide the Earth towards a better future.

This process, however, is not concerned with the recently deceased passing on personal messages from the afterlife. The messages are believed to be from other, alien races, passing on their wisdom to a select few on Earth in preparation for contact. The messages are most commonly received through telepathy or automatic writing, but a few very rare channellers have experienced the alien beings speaking through their bodies.

These new age channellers regard themselves as

able to "tune in" to these messages, much as we tune in the radio. They do this in much the same way as mediums do when contacting the spirit world, by entering a trance-like state which enables the energy of the "messenger" to flow through them.

The majority of such messages are peaceful in nature, but there has been a steady increase in ecological issues and prophecies about the fate of the Earth.

Channelling started in the twentieth century, through the pioneering work of Edgar Cayce. Cayce claimed to have been able to access the "Akashic records" – the cosmic memory bank of the thoughts and actions of all souls. He was not a channeller himself, though. He claimed to be completely unaware of his own powers, since they came to him only when he was in a trance. But he became a well-publicized healer. Apparently, he could use telepathy, a power he gained from a being from another dimension, to look into the body of a sick patient, no matter how many miles separated them. He would then prescribe treatment for them, usually involving rare herbs and strange diets. Over a period of forty years, he is believed to have cured 30,000 patients using these methods.

One of the earliest and best known of the channellers was Jane Roberts, who channelled an entity called "Seth". Her first encounter with this entity was on 9 September 1963, as she was sitting quietly in her living room. She suddenly felt her brain spark into action, and fill her head with amazing thoughts:

> "*A fantastic avalanche of radical, new ideas burst into my head with tremendous force, as if my skull were some sort of receiving station turned up to*

> *unbearable volume. It was as if the physical world*
> *were really tissue-paper thin, hiding infinite*
> *dimensions of reality, and I was suddenly flung*
> *through the tissue paper with a huge, ripping*
> *sound. My body sat at the table, my hands furiously*
> *scribbling down the words and ideas that flashed*
> *through my head."*

Jane felt that she had become possessed by another being, and during this onslaught she automatically wrote 100 pages of bizarre ideas that were not her own thoughts. The being announced that it was called Seth, and it continued to vocalize the following four messages:

1. We create our own reality;
2. Our point of power is the present;
3. We are not at the mercy of the subconscious, nor are we helpless; and
4. We are all gods couched in creaturehood.

Over the next few weeks, Jane was granted incredible psychic powers by Seth, allegedly including telepathy, clairvoyance, dream recall and precognitive dreams. Jane's channelling of Seth continued from this first encounter until her own death, twenty-one years later, and produced reams of material, including five books which she published about her experiences with this strange entity.

Seth described himself, through Jane, as "an energy personality essence no longer focused in physical reality". He in turn was part of a greater energy force known as "All That Is", most commonly thought of as God in the Western world. Seth claimed that everyone was a part of All That Is, and he offered a definition of the soul. Seth told Jane that the soul was a "power-house of probabilities or probable actions, a grouping of non-physical consciousness that nevertheless knows itself as an identity". He then went on to describe how, after death, the disembodied soul has a form that seems physical but is invisible to living humans and is endowed with superhuman powers. "It can do anything that you can do now in your dreams. Therefore it flies, goes through solid objects, and is moved directly by your will, taking you, say, from one location to another as you may think of these locations."

Jane Roberts's experiences seemed to open the floodgates for other new age channellers, who started to come forward with accounts of their own encounters. Many also claim to have channelled Seth, and others have allegedly channelled anything from angels to alien beings from other planets, times and dimensions. The message, however, always seems to be the same: tales of ageless wisdom, an immortal soul and some form of "All That Is" or God-like energy source. Sometimes the channelled material offers advice on daily living, career moves, love affairs and health issues. At other times, the advice given allows glimpses into the past or future.

One of the most celebrated new age channellers is Lyssa Royal Holt. Lyssa is an internationally recognized author, lecturer and channel. While studying for her degree in psychology, she developed an interest in hypnosis, and learned how to place herself in altered states of consciousness for the purpose of stress management. This ability helped her to develop the necessary skills for her later development as a channel.

Lyssa performs what she calls semi-conscious channelling. This means that she does not leave her body, but does go into an altered state of consciousness. She describes the experience as follows:

> "It feels like I am asleep and dreaming and when I wake up it feels dreamlike. I don't often remember what I've channelled. I chose to do it in a semi-conscious state because I didn't want to leave my body and miss all the fun! I wanted to benefit from the information and the interactions with the audience."

Lyssa has channelled more than one entity, but her main channel is "Sasha". Sasha, Lyssa claims, is a Pleiadian female. She has straight, shoulder-length hair, with large, almond-shaped light-brown eyes. She apparently looks very much like an Earth female, but her ears are slightly lower on her head than ours are. Sasha was born in the Pleiades in the twenty-fourth century, some years from now. Sasha claims to have a physical body, but not in the way that we know physicality. She says her reality lies in the fourth dimension, meaning that her body is made up mainly of light. In her channelling, Lyssa has been given information about the future of the Earth. Sasha has explained through Lyssa that we on Earth will go through a difficult time as old paradigms break down to make way for the new, but that the experience does not need to be traumatic if we take responsibility for ourselves as a species and for our home planet. In short, we must become more environmentally aware. Lyssa feels that the proof of the existence of Sasha lies in the many revelations that she has channelled and which have come true. She channelled a great deal of information which she collected into a book, *Preparing for Contact*, and is finding that much of what was spoken of by Sasha is now actually happening.

Lyssa also works for the SETI (Search for Extra-Terrestrial Intelligence) programme. Sasha had told her that soon Lyssa and others involved in the programme would begin to see patterns in their contact research, that they would begin to see the same type of low-level contacts happening over and over again. She then said that other research teams would have the same results. After Lyssa's book was published, this started to happen. For example, Lyssa and her fellow researchers began to see what looked like satellites traversing the sky and making sudden strange changes in trajectory. When the researchers began to signal to these mysterious objects using extremely powerful halogen lights, they signalled back. This has now become a recognized predictability pattern, and other research teams throughout the world have begun to experience the same phenomenon.

J. Z. Knight has been perhaps the most successful channeller, certainly in terms of the amount of cash that she has generated for herself through her alleged ability. Knight claims to be the conduit for "Ramtha, the Enlightened One", a 35,000-year-old warrior spirit who, while on Earth in corporeal form, thousands of years ago, apparently conquered the legendary city of Atlantis. Knight became a media celebrity with her channelling, and has a host of followers who believe her (or rather, Ramtha's) every word. She has even been followed by her devotees to the Pacific North

West in order to avoid the catalogue of disasters predicted for humanity by the warrior spirit.

Knight performs her channellings on stage, and the message that comes across from Ramtha is a common theme: "Love what you are. Love the god that you are. Embrace the wind, and the willow, and the water, for it is the creation of your importance, and be at peace," is a typical message given out at one of her seminars. Ramtha has also spoken of an advanced civilization living at the centre of the Earth. The entity has also predicted that Mother Nature will rid the Earth of homosexuals (whatever happened to "love what you are?"), that California will sink into the sea after a series of earthquakes and that Florida will also disappear off the world map.

Ramtha and Knight have achieved cult status, with over 3,000 devoted followers believing every vague word spouted on stage, tape and video by Ms Knight. For many followers, believing in Ramtha works. As one follower put it,

"I watched great changes come over people around me – people who lacked hope came alive again."

Perhaps the admission fee of $1,000 to one of Knight's seminars is not so steep after all – or could it be the fact that some people's lives are so devoid of purpose and significance that even the ridiculous, if it offers meaning and direction, appears reasonable, if not profound?

So what does the scientific community make of these new age channellers? To date, the scientists have had little interest in the phenomenon; even parapsychology has taken small note of the channellers. What little notice has been taken has come from psychologists and religious groups. There is some speculation that channelling is the product of hypnosis. Carl Raschke, a professor of religion, believes that channelling may involve both the self-hypnosis of the channeller and of the audience. Raschke theorizes that channellers put themselves into a self-induced hypnotic state that somehow mesmerizes an audience already prone to the belief that God is everywhere. Another professor, David Spiegel from Stanford University, describes channelling as "a fantasy acted out in a very intense way".

A handful of investigators see channelling as a form of mental disorder similar to multiple personality disorder (see Chapter 11). This theory supports the notion that channellers are suffering from multiple personality disorder, but that they are mistaking one of their own personalities for an entity exterior to their own self. In other words, new age channellers are deluded – mad. Visions of unwordly entities are certainly strange to the majority of us, but do those who experience them deserve the label of "insane"? Are channellers simply attuned to a different reality? Dr John Beahrs, a psychiatrist from Oregon, points to a theory first spoken of by a psychic researcher, Walter Franklin Prince, called "coconsciousness".

Beahrs defines coconsciousness as "the existence within a single human organism of more than one consciously experiencing psychological entity, each with its own identity and selfhood, relatively separate and distinct from other entities". This closely resembles multiple personality disorder, but Beahrs believes that coconsciousness is a natural state rather than a mental problem. If so, the ability to tap into another, higher consciousness might be something which we can all do. This is certainly something that Lyssa Royal believes, and she gives seminars which train people to channel for themselves.

The basic problem remains, however, that there are several theories which try to explain this curious phenomenon, but, as with so many aspects of psychic powers, no proof. It comes down, eventually, to a question of personal belief, in much the same way as religion. You either believe in the phenomenon, or you don't, and no amount of theorizing is likely to change your opinion. Some sceptics have been converted by their own experiences of channellers, in much the same way as some believers have lost their faith in channelling because of the number of charlatans who pretend to have the ability in order to make easy money. As one critic of J.Z. Knight put it:

> *"It doesn't take a rocket scientist to figure out that the likelihood of a 35,000-year-old Cro-Magnon ghost suddenly appearing in a kitchen to a homemaker to reveal profundities about centres and voids, self-love and guilt-free living, or love and peace, is close to zero."*

It does seem strange that channellers who claim to be conduits for messages from alien species have only appeared on the scene in the last fifty years or so. The world is becoming obsessed with UFOlogy and the belief that we are not alone in the universe – you only have to look at the output of the film industry over the same period of time to judge how fascinated we are by the prospect of visitations from other planets. Perhaps these new age channellers are simply capitalizing on the latest fad. If not, and they genuinely are communicating with entities from other realms and dimensions, then why are only a select few chosen by the aliens as their messengers? If they wish for humans to progress to a higher state of consciousness, they are doing a poor job of convincing us to do so. Six billion people will need to be convinced that that is what they must do, and a handful of channellers will be hard pressed to do that on their own. Perhaps, in the words of H. G. Wells, "minds immeasurably superior to ours" are not at work in the universe after all.

Psychic Voyages

Out-of-the-body experiences

The human mind finds it extremely hard to cope with the reality of death. For the vast majority of people on the planet, the coping mechanism used is a belief that there is a part of everyone which is immortal. Death is simply the expiry of the physical body, or to put it another way, death is the soul leaving the body. But is it possible for the soul to leave the body momentarily, without it dying? Many people believe that they have experienced such a phenomenon, which psychic investigators now refer to as an OOBE or out-of-the-body experience.

Fifty years after Charles Lindbergh made his historic transatlantic flight, he made public what he believed to be an out-of-the-body experience that he claims happened during the twenty-second hour of the flight. When his plane was enveloped in a dense fog, and he was under great stress, Lindbergh suddenly felt himself becoming as formless as a ghost:

> *"I existed independently of time and matter. I felt myself departing from my body as I imagine a spirit would depart – emanating into the cockpit, extending through the fuselage as though no frame*

or fabric walls were there, angling upward, outward, until I reformed in an awareness far distant from the human form I left in a fast-flying transatlantic plane. But I remained connected to my body through a long-extended strand, a strand so tenuous that it could have been severed by a breath."

Lindbergh knew that people would explain away his OOBE as being the result of extreme fatigue and stress. In his autobiography, he sought to disclaim this idea stating that, "my visions are easily explained away through reason, but the longer I live, the more limited I believe rationality to be". A sentiment echoed by many a psychic over the years.

Astral projection, ESP projection or OOBE, whatever one wishes to label the experience in which a person leaves his or her physical body and appears to view the external world from a different position, has been widely reported in both psychic and medical journals, and appears to be a relatively common experience. The circumstances in which an OOBE occurs do, however, vary considerably. Stress does indeed seem to be a common factor; many people have reported OOBEs when undergoing an operation, during or after an accident or when seriously ill. But there are also many other cases of people merely asleep, or performing everyday tasks such as shopping, when the experience occurred.

In the vast majority of accounts given by those who claim to have had an OOBE, the initial sensation that they have felt has been indistinguishable from the ordinary state, except for a feeling of positive well-being and weightlessness. Many have reported that

The soul departing the body during an OOBE.

they felt that their "astral" form was still connected to their body by some form of thin cord, enabling them to return to the physical body at any time.

The astral body has been the subject of scrutiny for centuries. In yogic teaching (see Chapter 7), there are eight *siddhis* which can be acquired through meditation. The sixth siddhi is "flying in the sky", meaning, in some definitions, levitation, and in others, astral projection. All modern and ancient religions refer to the existence of the soul, and make direct references to the astral body. It is this belief that has led to the modern idea that it is wrong to wake a sleepwalker, for fear that to do so would prevent the soul, or astral body, from returning.

The fact remains that the OOBE is not a Western phenomenon. It crosses all cultures. No particular ethnic group or nationality seems more or less prone to OOBEs than any other and reports of the phenomenon have been collected from every culture and race. In 1978, Professor Shiels of the University of Wisconsin published the results of a cross-cultural study of beliefs in OOBEs. He had collected data from nearly seventy non-Western cultures, which revealed a belief in the phenomenon from about 95 per cent of them. Professor Shiels noted in his report that "the near-universality of OOBE beliefs and the *consistency* of the beliefs is striking". Not only, therefore, have all cultures experienced OOBEs, but the manner of the experiences seems to be universal also.

The whole subject of such psychic voyages has become the subject of scientific investigation, and there seems to be little middle ground between two bodies of thought. The sceptics simply dismiss OOBEs as mere hallucinations or even fraud. The advocates, and those who have experienced OOBEs, maintain that the incidents involve a much stronger sense of reality than is usually experienced in dreams or hallucinations. They also state, quite rightly, that the experiences of OOBEs throughout different countries and cultures are all so incredibly similar that the phenomenon cannot be dismissed as the dreams and hallucinations of a gullible few. Dr Charles Tart, a psychical researcher, summed up this view succinctly:

> *"Because of its apparently universal distribution across cultures and throughout history, an out-of-the-body experience constitutes what the psychiatrist Carl Jung termed an 'archetypal' experience – an experience potentially available to many members of the human race simply by virtue of being human."*

The phenomenon is incredibly common. Researchers have estimated that anything between 15 and 20 per cent of the human race will experience an OOBE at some point in their lifetime. But there have been a few remarkable individuals who claim that they can actually induce an OOBE, and thereby travel to the astral plane seemingly at will.

One such gentleman was Hugh Calloway. He was born in 1885, during a time when Spiritualism was at the height of its popularity both in the United Kingdom and America. He was a sickly child who was prone to having vivid dreams and nightmares. His dreams always started the same way, with spawn-like, blue, vibrating circles. If these circles then morphed into small inkpots, then he would dream peacefully, but if they turned into tiny faces with evil, piercing eyes, he would suffer a terrible nightmare. Calloway first believed that he had psychic ability when he found that he could will the blue circles to form into the inkpots. Calloway's parents both died within six months of each other, when he was around the age of thirteen. He was initially terrified of death, but soon came to the view that should he die, he would be reunited with his mother and father. As he grew older, he started to have intense dreams about his mother, and when he woke, he would be convinced that he had been in her presence.

As time passed, Calloway's dreams became more and more intense, offering him clear insight. While a student at Southampton University, he dreamed that he was standing on the pavement outside his dormitory. He then began to develop a power whereby he could rise off the ground and pass through walls, although he was always called back to his body by some unknown force that gave him a crippling headache if he tried to resist it. Calloway decided one night that he would, despite the headaches, try to break free from the force that always called him back to his body. He succeeded, and the pain in his head melted away. However, when he attempted to return to his physical body he found that he couldn't, until he used all his will-power to force his astral form back into his flesh. He then found that he could not move at all. After some time, lying paralysed, Calloway used all his strength to move one finger and, over the period of a few hours, finally managed to overcome his paralysis.

Up to this point, all Calloway's experiences could simply be dismissed as dreams and illusions until, that is, he decided to share his story with his fellow students. Two of his friends at university reported that they too had had OOBEs or "psychic travels" as they put it, and one night the three of them decided that their astral forms should meet on the university commons. Calloway and one of his friends made the journey successfully, and both woke up the next morning to report that they had indeed met on the commons as they had planned, in a dream.

Calloway's girlfriend, Elsie, was very sceptical about his claims. One night they had an argument about it, and Calloway severely castigated her for her disbelief, calling her a "narrow-minded little ignoramus". Elsie decided to show Calloway that she was far from that. Later that night, Calloway was lying in his bed when he suddenly saw a cloud of bluish light, at the centre of which stood Elsie in her nightgown. He lay there trans-fixed for a period, then called out her name, and she vanished.

The following day, Calloway met Elsie, and before he could tell her of his experience from the night before, she told him of her travels:

> *"I did come to you, I really did. I went to sleep, willing that I would, and all at once I was there. This morning I knew just how everything was in your room."*

Elsie had never before been to Calloway's room, but she then told him exactly what was in it and how it was laid out, including the fact that Calloway had been lying on the left side of a double bed with his eyes open, staring at her, when she had made her appear-ance. Calloway was now convinced that he was not mad, and that he might even be on the verge of an amazing discovery which could affect the history of mankind. He decided to intensify his astral travels, and see just how far from his body he could go.

During the 1920s, Calloway chronicled his experiences in a British psychical journal. He told of how he had found himself in the middle of a glittering, oriental city beside the sculpture of a huge, kneeling black elephant. On another occasion, he reported that he had attempted to travel astrally to a Tibetan temple, but had found himself in a torture chamber, bound to a rack and being forced to reveal his true identity to his tormentors. When he refused, he was sent back immediately to his physical body. He also reported that he had learned how to induce a trance without actually falling asleep, leaving his body through a gateway in his pineal gland. The pineal gland is located within the brain, and is thought by many scientists to be directly connected to out-of-the-body experiences. By 1938, when Calloway published his book detailing his astral travels, he had been largely dismissed as a crank. Furthermore, his experiences had been eclipsed by the accounts of a young American, who had published a book entitled *The Projection of the Astral Body* in 1929.

Sylvan Joseph Muldoon was an eager proponent of all things spiritual and psychic from a very early age. In 1927 he read a book on astral projection in which the author stated that a Frenchman, Charles Lancelin, was the leading expert on the subject. Muldoon wrote to the author, Hereward Carrington, and told him that his own experiences far outweighed anything that Lancelin had himself spoken about. Carrington was intrigued, and offered to be the co-author on Muldoon's soon-to-be-published book. In the book, Muldoon relates his experiences back to when he was twelve and had his first OOBE. While on a camping holiday, Muldoon had woken suddenly from a deep sleep, to find that his body was acting in a very strange way:

> *"My entire rigid body (I thought it was my physical, but it was my astral) commenced vibrating at a great rate of speed, in an up-and-down direction . . . Then the sense of hearing began to function, and that of sight followed. When able to see, I was more than astonished: I was floating in the air, rigidly horizontal a few feet above the bed . . . I was uprighted and placed standing upon the floor of the room . . . Then I managed to turn around. There was another me lying quietly on the bed. My two identical bodies were joined by means of an elastic-like cable which extended across the space of probably six feet which separated us . . . My first thought was that I had died during sleep."*

Muldoon then went on to describe how his astral form drifted into his mother's room, and tried to wake her. His hands passed straight through his mother's body, however, and he became terrified that he had, in fact, died. His astral body began to sob, until the cord which linked it to his physical body suddenly jerked, and he was pulled back into the flesh. He described this reunification as an intensely painful experience:

> *"Every muscle in the physical body jerked, and a penetrating pain, as if I had been split open from head to foot, shot through me. I was physically alive again, as amazed as fearful. I had been conscious throughout the entire occurrence."*

Muldoon was initially petrified by his experience, but over the years he became accustomed to his "other self". He had hundreds of OOBEs, the most celebrated of which took place in 1924. He had returned home after a walk, and had locked himself in his room for a nap. Soon he felt his body going numb, which he by now recognized as an early symptom of an oncoming OOBE. Seconds later, he felt his astral body rise up. He wandered around his house for a while, then went outside. Once outside, he was suddenly carried at immense speed to a farmhouse that he had never seen before, where he saw four people sitting round a table. One of them was a young girl, sewing a black dress. He watched her for a while, explored the room they were in, then was pulled back to his physical body.

Several weeks later he was shocked when he bumped into the girl his astral body had seen. He asked her where she lived and she, naturally presuming that he was mad, refused to tell him. So Muldoon described where she lived to her, in explicit detail. The girl was stunned, and asked how he knew. Muldoon explained, they became better acquainted, and he went to visit the farmhouse. It was exactly as he had seen it during his out-of-the-body experience. It was also fifteen miles from his home, where his physical body had lain during his first "visit" to the farmhouse.

The third of the famous astral projectors differed from the other two in that he had his first out-of-the-body experience at the age of forty-three. Robert Monroe had never had any links with the Spiritualist movement, which the other two had, and was generally thought of as a very normal, level-headed American businessman. His first experience, like the other two, was far from pleasant. In his own words, he was gripped by a "severe, iron-hard cramp, which extended across my diaphragm or solar plexus area just under my ribcage. It was a solid band of unyielding ache". He initially suspected that it was food poisoning, but none of the other members of his family had been affected, and they had all eaten the same food. It eventually waned, after ten and a half hours of agony, but returned three weeks later. For the next six weeks Monroe experienced these attacks, which always happened as he was lying down to sleep or rest, and disappeared when he sat upright. He consulted his doctor, and described symptoms such as the sensation of a ring of sparks, starting at his head, sweeping down to his toes and then back to his head, over and over again. When the rings passed over his head, he felt a great roaring, and could actually feel the vibrations in his brain. He felt that he was becoming schizophrenic. Monroe's doctor assured him that this was not the case, but gave him a thorough medical examination. He was confirmed as not being an epileptic, nor of having a brain tumour, and was diagnosed as perfectly healthy. The doctor prescribed that he lose some weight and try to get more sleep.

One night the vibrations returned and, as Monroe was waiting for them to pass, his arm brushed against the floor, and he pressed his fingers into the rug lying there. His fingers passed straight through the rug, and through the floor beneath it. He continued to push, and his fingers felt a small chip of wood, a bent nail and some sawdust, finally splashing into some water. Monroe was obviously bewildered, as he claims that he was fully conscious throughout the experience:

"I was wide awake. I could see the moonlit landscape through the window. I could feel myself lying on the bed, the covers over my body, the pillow under my head, my chest rising and falling as I breathed. The vibrations were still present, but to a lesser degree. How could I be awake in all other respects and still 'dream' that my arm was stuck down through the floor?"

A perplexing question indeed, but his experiences became even stranger over the next few months. In another "attack", Monroe was again lying on his bed, when he became aware of something rubbing against his shoulder. He thought it was the wall, but as he looked around, he realized that it was in fact the ceiling. His account of what happened on this occasion will seem all too familiar to anyone reading who has experienced an OOBE for themselves:

"I was floating against the ceiling, bouncing gently with any movement I made. I rolled in the air, startled, and looked down. There, in the dim light below me, was the bed. There were two figures lying in the bed. To the right was my wife. Beside her was someone else. I looked more closely, and the shock was intense. I was the someone on the bed. Here I was, there was my body. I was dying, this was death and I wasn't ready to die. Desperately, like a diver, I swooped down to my body and dove in. I then felt the bed and the covers, and when I opened my eyes, I was looking at the room from the perspective of my bed."

Monroe sincerely felt that he was going to die, and

he went to see a friend of his who was a psychologist. He explained to his friend that he was not ready to die, that he wanted to live longer, and his friend, to an extent, put his mind at ease. He explained how in Eastern religions, many fakirs and yogi actually practised what Monroe had experienced, and could do it whenever they wanted. What Monroe had experienced was not, he said, a foreboding of death, but an astral projection, an out-of-the-body experience. Monroe felt relieved, but also incredibly curious, and he decided to keep detailed records of his journeys, complete with information about the places he visited. He became a master of the "affliction", and eventually claimed to have travelled between three different dimensions, which he called Locales I, II and III.

Locale I was the material world, the one which we are all familiar with, and while on this plane Monroe stayed fairly close to his own home. Locale II, however, was a plane of existence that very few claim to have visited. Monroe described it as:

"... *a non-material environment with laws of motion and matter only remotely related to the physical world. It has depth and dimensions incomprehensible to the finite, conscious mind. In this vastness lie all of the aspects we attribute to heaven and hell, which are but part of Locale II. It is inhabited, if that is the word, by entities with various degrees of intelligence with whom communication is possible. Superseding all appears to be one prime law. Locale II is a state of being where that which we label thought is the wellspring of existence. It is the vital creative force that produces energy, assembles 'matter' into form, and provides channels of perception and communication. In this environment, no mechanical supplements are found. You think movement and it is fact."*

The third location, Locale III, was very similar to Locale I. Monroe claimed that it was very similar to the physical world we know, except that it had evolved on a different technology. There was, apparently, no electricity – the inhabitants of Locale III seemed to rely on some other power, which Monroe described as nuclear. The interesting thing about this place though, was that Monroe apparently met his double – as he put it, "the 'I' who lives 'there'". Monroe claims that he inhabited the body of his other self, an architect who lived in a boarding house and rode to work on a bus.

This all sounds rather incredible. Monroe himself was equally perplexed and intrigued by the whole thing, and offered his own explanations for the two other planes of existence. For example, he thought that Locale III might be some form of race memory of a physical earth which existed before history began, or another earth located somewhere else in the universe. He even speculated that it might be "an antimatter duplicate of this physical earth-world where we are the same but different, bonded together unit for unit by a force beyond our present comprehension". In his book *Journeys Out of the Body*, Monroe made meticulous notes about the other worlds. He noted down the temperatures there, the percentage of the days shared between light and dark and physical descriptions of the landscape. In time, he left his job as an advertising executive and devoted his life to investigating OOBEs and other psychic phenomena. He went on to found the Monroe Institute for Applied Sciences in Virginia, to teach others how to achieve an OOBE, using audio tapes which he claimed were designed to synchronize the electrical impulses of the left and right hemispheres of the brain.

The problem with all three of these psychic voyagers is that there is no proof. Parapsychologist Charles Tart defined an OOBE as:

> *"an event in which the experiencer seems to perceive some portion of some environment which could not possibly be perceived from where his physical body is known to be at the time; and knows at the time that he is not dreaming or fantasizing."*

This definition also matches the experience anyone has of listening on the telephone or watching the television. The problem with all three astral travellers described above is that it is impossible to know for certain that one is "not dreaming or fantasizing". Given the extremely complex nature of the human brain, it cannot be said with any real certainty that sensory malfunctions do not occur that give the strong impression of being real, while in actual fact they have all been just "in the mind".

Scientific research

The central problem with trying to assess the reality of the phenomenon over the years has been the lack of subjects to test. The three cases above had, until fairly recently, remained more or less alone in their efforts to validate the existence of OOBEs, even though reports of the phenomenon were widespread throughout the world. In the 1960s, two well-respected British scientists conducted extensive surveys into OOBEs, in an effort scientifically to prove or disprove the phenomenon.

Celia Green founded the Institute of Psychophysical Research at Oxford. She sent out an appeal through the national press, asking for details from anyone who thought that they had had an OOBE, and received responses from 326 people of all different ages. Of those, sixty had had only one OOBE, and the remainder had experienced more than one. The statistics showed that those who had had more than one OOBE had almost exclusively experienced their very first one as a child, whereas those who had only experienced one OOBE had experienced it between the ages of fifteen and thirty-five. As a rule, the incidence of OOBE journeys reduced with age. Most of the cases that Celia Green investigated were nowhere near as intense as those experienced by the famous trio above. One example concerned a waitress who, having worked a very long shift at the restaurant at which she was employed, experienced what she believed to be a minor OOBE on her journey home. Her report seemed to suggest a slightly altered state of consciousness, probably brought on by fatigue, but nevertheless, a total awareness of another, astral, self:

> *"I remember feeling so fatigued that I wondered if I'd make it. The next I registered was of hearing the sound of my heels very hollowly and I looked down and watched myself walk round the bend of the*

street. I saw myself very clearly – it was a summer evening and I was wearing a sleeveless, shantung dress. I remember thinking 'so that's how I look to other people'."

At the same time, Robert Crookall, principal geologist at the Institute of Geological Sciences, was collecting data on OOBEs, because of his own fascination with psychic phenomena. He analysed nearly 1000 accounts from people all over the world, which he documented in several books. He noticed a recurring theme throughout the global experiences that he recorded. In the vast majority of cases, people who had experienced an OOBE reported that the dissociation of the astral body frequently began at the extremities, the hands and feet, and finished at the head. Many reported that they blacked out or heard clicking sounds at the moment when they first became completely separated from their physical body. These consistencies applied to cases drawn from all over the world, detailing the OOBEs of people who had never met each other, yet they seemed to be sharing many similar experiences.

The data collected individually by Green and Crookall came to the attention of Dr Charles Tart at the University of Virginia, and he decided to perform a series of experiments under laboratory conditions to investigate out-of-the-body experiences. His main subject during these tests called himself "Mr X" to hide his identity, and it eventually came out that he was in fact Robert Monroe, the man who had apparently travelled to the three different planes of existence, outlined above. Dr Tart obviously thought that if anyone could summon up an out-of-the-body experience under test conditions, it would be Monroe.

Monroe was placed in a room where he was linked up to machines which monitored his heartbeat, rapid eye movements, brain wave activity and respiration. Dr Tart requested that Monroe induce an OOBE, then astrally project himself into an adjoining room. Once inside the other room, he was to read a randomly selected five-digit number which had been placed on a shelf that was high enough to ensure that it could not be seen by normal vision. Monroe would have to "float" up to see it. Unused to his surroundings, and decidedly uncomfortable, Monroe failed to induce an OOBE on the first seven attempts, but managed successfully on the eighth. He left his physical body and visited the room next door, as requested, but did not see the random numbers. He did, however, notice that the laboratory technician who should have been in the room was absent, and floated out into the corridor, where he saw the technician. When he woke up, Monroe told Dr Tart that he had seen the technician in the corridor, talking to a man whom he did not recognize. The technician confirmed that she had indeed been in the corridor at the time, talking with her husband.

Dr Tart was unconvinced by his experiments with Monroe, but sufficiently curious to continue with his research. He soon found another subject, who was a student at his university, and whom he called "Miss Z". Miss Z had claimed to have on average three OOBEs every week, usually waking in the middle of the night to find her astral form floating near the ceiling. Dr Tart performed similar tests on Miss Z to those he had conducted with Robert Monroe. This time, Dr Tart would place the five random numbers out of sight on a small shelf above Miss Z's bed, several feet above her head.

On the fourth night of the tests, at nearly six o'clock in the morning, the electroencephalograph to which Miss Z was connected registered disturbed brain wave activity that represented neither clear-cut sleep nor waking. Shortly after six o'clock, Miss Z called in the technician and reported that she had had an OOBE, and had successfully read the numbers, 25132. This was the exact target sequence. Coincidence was ruled out by the fact that to guess these five numbers in sequence would require odds in excess of 100,000 to 1. When Dr Tart checked the other monitors, he found that during the time of the OOBE, Miss Z's heart rate and brain wave patterns did not slow down, and that there was no sign of rapid eye movement, all of which suggests that she had not been dreaming. But did Dr Tart's experiments conclude that OOBEs existed? In a strictly scientific sense, no. Miss Z could have read the digits by clairvoyance, without her supposed astral form leaving her physical body. The next question for the scientists then was how to differentiate OOBE sight from extra-sensory perception.

Dr Karlis Osis of the American Society for Psychical Research was convinced of the phenomenon of OOBEs, and decided to design an experiment which would prove that clairvoyance was not present in an OOBE. Clairvoyant sight supposedly has no limitations, unlike normal sight and OOBE vision. Osis used as his subject an artist and now famous psychical researcher, Ingo Swann. In the experiments, Swann would sit on a chair, hooked up to similar machines as in the Tart experiments, and induce an OOBE. Osis had placed certain objects in a box on a platform suspended from the ceiling, out of Swann's reach and sight. Swann had to leave his physical body and, on return, describe to Osis what was in the box. On one occasion, during these experiments, Swann accurately, and in very great detail, described two intricate drawings that were in the box. But the proof, for Osis, that this was an out-of-the-body experience, came with a failed attempt. Swann had left his physical body but, on approaching the box, noticed that the little light inside it was not on. He could only make out vague forms, but could not read anything that was written on the paper in the box. This suggested that his sight was indeed limited in the same way as normal sight. Clairvoyance would most likely not have been put off by dim light.

But Osis was still not satisfied with his experiments. He wanted concrete evidence to prove that some form of astral self actually leaves the physical self during an alleged OOBE. To do this, Osis began a new series of experiments using a specially adapted optical image device. The machine was about 3 feet by 2 feet (914 mm by 610 mm), with a viewing hole in one side. When looking through the hole, you could see a coloured picture lying on one of four quadrants. The image in the machine was in fact generated by a random number generator, and was projected via a series of mirrors and coloured filters. Osis's hypothesis was that someone having an OOBE would simply see a picture, whereas a clairvoyant would detect the mirrors and filters instead of the optical illusion.

Osis had another subject for this series of experiments, Alex Tanous, a man who had a reputation as a psychic, and who had been used several times in police investigations to catch criminals. In 197 tests using

Osis's new optical machinery, Tanous correctly identified the image on 114 occasions. The other machinery
attached to Tanous showed remarkable brain wave
activity on the occasions when he was correct.

For all his efforts, Osis has never proved for certain
that the astral body exists. True, he has come up with
some amazing results which positively suggest that the
phenomenon exists, but sceptics will still argue that
his proof is far from conclusive. Psychologists
maintain that alleged OOBEs stem from a mental state
called "lucid dreaming", where a person who is asleep
and dreaming realizes that they are dreaming, and
thus believes that he or she is out of their body.
Psychical researchers disagree strongly with this point
of view. In all the experiments using medical technology to monitor heart rates and brain wave activity,
results have indicated that while subjects have been
very relaxed, their brain wave patterns have not shown
results associated with sleep. If not asleep, how could
they be dreaming? The only conclusions to be drawn
are that they are either experiencing an altered state of
consciousness or are indeed experiencing out-of-the-
body phenomena.

Whatever the reason, OOBEs usually have a
profound effect on those experiencing them. Many
people who have had the experience become
convinced of other worlds or dimensions, while others
are assured that there is life after death. Those who
believe in the latter have often experienced a different
form of OOBE, the near-death experience, which shall
be examined in the next chapter. The truth is that
people from all over the world, regardless of age, sex,
race or culture, claim to have experienced an out-of-
the-body experience. The weight of evidence provided

by these global tales must surely not be dismissed as idle fantasy by the scientific community, however sceptical. It is the one area of psychic phenomena that could, after all, prove once and for all what mankind craves so badly: the confirmation that there is life after death.

The Search for Immortality
●●●●●●●●●●●●●●●●●●●●●●●●●●●●●●●●

Near-death experiences

It was a stiflingly hot July night in 1918, near the village of Fossalta, on the Italian front. All around the sounds of the war raged on relentlessly, and the only light in the moonless sky was from enemy fire. Crouched in a filthy trench with his comrades was a young officer from the US Ambulance Corps, listening intently to the rapid fire of the machine guns and the pounding of the mortars. His ears tuned in to the all-too-familiar whistle of a mortar shell hurtling through the air. Closer and closer it came. A second later, fire exploded around him. Shrapnel scattered through the air, piercing his body, splintering his legs. The soldier felt his life ebbing away. Lying there, he sensed his spirit leaving his body, as if he were dying.

The soldier who was so horrifically injured during the horrors of World War I was the famous writer, Ernest Hemingway. He believed that, on the verge of death, he experienced a phenomenon whereby his spirit left his body, only to be wrenched back due to the life-saving efforts of his comrades. In his novel, *A Farewell to Arms*, he described his near-death experience in an episode in which the fictional character Frederick Henry is severely wounded and on the point of death:

> "*I tried to breathe but my breath would not come. I felt myself rush bodily out of myself and out and out and out and all the time bodily in the wind. I went out swiftly, all of myself, and I knew I was dead and that it had been a mistake to think you just died. Then I floated, and instead of going on I felt myself slide back. I breathed and I was back.*"

During December 1943, an army private named George Ritchie developed a life-threatening strain of influenza. He was hospitalized due to the seriousness of his illness, and one night his temperature reached 106.5°F (41°C). He felt dizzy and disorientated, his surroundings became a blur, then suddenly, darkness and silence. Ritchie thought he had passed out, and when he woke up he was on a strange bed in a small room. He was scheduled to leave for another town that day and, in a panic, he leapt from his bed to get ready, feeling much better. He looked about the room but could not see his uniform or his belongings and when he looked back at the bed, there was a young man lying just where he had been. Private Ritchie shivered and ran from the room out into the hallway. A sergeant was walking towards him, and Ritchie addressed him:

"Excuse me, sergeant, you haven't seen the ward boy for this unit, have you?" But the sergeant did not answer or even seem to notice that Ritchie was there. He walked on, apparently passing straight through Ritchie.

The next thing Ritchie knew he was outside the hospital, still wearing only his pyjamas, but not feeling the cold. It was dark and he was moving extremely fast, as though he was flying through the air. Ritchie willed himself to slow down, and "landed" on a street corner in a town he did not recognize. He stood agape as people walked past without seeing him, and to regain his composure, he leant against a lamp-post. His body passed straight through it. Ritchie knew that he had to get back to his physical body. He could only think of his appointment, and how he would miss it in his current form. He flew back to the hospital even faster than he had left it, and when he got there, he ran from room to room, looking for his physical form. He eventually spotted a left hand which was wearing an onyx and gold fraternity ring – his ring – but noticed that the body was covered with a sheet. He knew that this meant that he was dead. Suddenly, the room was baked in an intense light, and a man formed purely from light appeared. Ritchie heard the words, "You are in the presence of the Son of God." At that exact moment, Ritchie's whole life, every event, conversation, thought and touch, passed in front of him as a series of pictures.

The next thing Ritchie knew, he had woken up, back in his physical body, alive. This rather amazed the doctor who had just signed his death certificate. An orderly who had been preparing Ritchie's body for the morgue had noticed very faint signs of life, and had called the doctor, who injected adrenaline directly into Ritchie's heart. He made a full recovery, in spite of the fact that he had not taken a breath for over nine minutes. He suffered no brain damage, even though, medically speaking, a brain starved of oxygen for this length of time would be expected to be severely damaged as a result. According to *CPR: Resuscitation of the arrested heart,* if the brain is starved of oxygen for five minutes or more, it is extremely likely that it will suffer damage.

Anecdotal evidence of such experiences can be sourced from all over the world, and from almost any point in history. Consider these next three accounts:

Bill had been in an accident, and was losing blood rapidly. When the bleeding wouldn't stop, he knew that he was dying:

> *"I was going, but I felt totally at peace. There was a golden kind of light, brighter than the sun, but it didn't hurt my eyes. I never wanted anything as much as to go into that light, but something or somebody – it felt like my dad, who died when I was a kid – communicated to me, 'It isn't your time. You must go back to finish what you have to do in your life.' The next thing I knew, I was slammed back into my body. It felt like a wet sock, and the pain was just awful."*

Marilyn had been taken to hospital after a severe heart attack. While in the emergency room, her pain suddenly stopped:

> *"All at once I just popped out of my body and floated up to the ceiling. I could see dust on top of the light fixtures, and I thought, 'Boy, somebody's going to catch it for this!' I could see doctors working on someone on the table, when all of a sudden I realized it was me – I mean, my body. I thought it was kind of silly they were working so hard. My family was waiting down the hall, and I*

wished my kids could stop crying; I wanted to let them know I was fine, but they couldn't hear me. Then it seemed I had to get back, that it was my job to take care of them, see them grow up okay."

Kurt described his experience as much more horrific. When his car stopped flipping after a crash, he felt as though he had been thrown into outer space:

"I was all alone, all by myself out in the universe. I could hear noises, sort of like moans, and I could see these figures in the distance. They seemed to be people wearing some kind of robe, and they were faceless. They were in torment. I don't know why I think that, except it just seemed that way. They were helpless and gesturing me to join them. Then I was realizing it would be like that for ever. Something – I don't know what – was sending me a message, something about making a choice. I don't really remember it exactly. Being there was so horrible I can't even describe it. That was fourteen years ago, and I still can't figure out what I ever did to deserve it."

What all these people have shared are near-death experiences. NDEs have occurred throughout history, in all parts of the world. It may even be possible that experiences such as these have helped to shape our ideas about heaven and hell. Whether that is true or not, NDEs certainly seem to point to the existence of an afterlife. Many people believe that the near-death experience *proves* the existence of an afterlife, that there is life after death in a literal sense. Others consider that the experience does not constitute proof of an afterlife, but that it suggests that some aspect of human consciousness (the psyche or soul) may be independent of the physical body, and may survive death. The more sceptical opinion is that the person who has undergone a near-death experience was hallucinating due to severe stress.

The near-death experience is among the most powerful experiences that a person can have, and it may permanently alter that person's perceptions of what is real and important in their life. The most extra-ordinary aspect of NDEs is that the underlying pattern seems not to be associated with the subject's culture, religion, race or education. There is no evidence to suggest that the type of experience is related to whether the person is religious or not, or has lived a "good" or "bad" life according to his or her society's standards.

An experience will often include the feeling of being out of the physical body, moving through darkness or a tunnel, encountering the presence of deceased loved ones and other entities, and an indescribable light or an oppressive darkness. Many people who have experienced a near-death experience say that they have glimpsed the pattern and meaning of life and the universe, or have been given information beyond ordinary human capabilities, a form of extra-sensory perception. For most people the experience is joyful beyond words, although there are cases where people have told of terrifying experiences.

No two NDEs are identical, but a definite pattern is evident throughout the vast majority of cases, and will generally include one or more of the following:

A feeling that the "self" has left the body and is hovering overhead.

Moving through a dark space or tunnel.

Experiencing incredibly intense emotions, ranging from utter bliss to abject terror.

Encountering a light, usually described as either golden or white, and being drawn to it as a thing of intense beauty; alternatively, it can be perceived as a reflection of the fires of hell.

Receiving a message along the lines of "it isn't your time yet", immediately before returning to the body.

Meeting others, including very often deceased friends or relatives or "beings of light".

Having your entire life flash before you, leading to revelations about what changes need to be made in your life.

Experiencing a sense of understanding everything, and of knowing how the universe works.

Reaching some form of boundary, a cliff or a body of water, and knowing that crossing it will mean that one cannot return back to life.

Receiving previously unknown information about one's own life, for example, that you were adopted or have a brother that you did not know about.

The decision to return to the body may be voluntary or involuntary. Some are thrust back, others choose to go back because of revelations about unfinished responsibilities.

Returning to the body and waking up.

Near-death investigators

Historically, near-death experiences have been viewed as religious events. Towards the end of the nineteenth century, however, a few researchers began to collect together anecdotes of such phenomena and group them together. This would eventually pave the way for a full scientific exploration of the near-death experience.

One of the first scientists to catalogue data on the phenomenon was Albert Heim, a professor of geology in Switzerland, and an avid mountain climber. Heim's interest in the area grew out of an experience that he had while climbing the Santis Mountain in the Swiss Alps in 1871. He slipped and fell from the edge of a cliff, and underwent a NDE on the mountainside. Describing the experience in his journal, he wrote:

> *"What followed was a series of singularly clear flashes of thought between a rapid, profuse succession of images that were sharp and distinct. I can perhaps compare it best to images from film sprung loose in a projector or with the rapid sequence of dream images. As though I looked out of the window of a high house, I saw myself as a seven-year-old boy going to school. Then I saw myself in the classroom with my beloved teacher Weisz, in fourth grade. I acted out my life as though I were an actor on stage, upon which I looked down as though from practically the highest gallery in the theatre ... Then I saw arching over me – my eyes were directed upwards – a beautiful blue heaven with small violet and rosy-red clouds. Then sounded solemn music, as though from an organ,*

in powerful chords. I felt myself go softly backwards into this magnificent heaven – without anxiety, without grief. It was a great, glorious moment!"

This experience completely changed Heim's life, and he went out to seek the reports of others who had had similar experiences. In 1892, he published an article that looked at the stories of more than thirty survivors of near-fatal climbing expeditions in the Alps. Heim was the first to identify many of the common elements of near-death experiences, and his publication led to a series of scientific experiments across the globe into the phenomenon.

One of the most celebrated of these new investigators was a physician at the Royal College of Science in Dublin, Sir William Barrett. His interest in the area was aroused by an experience related to him by his wife, and he began collecting reports of deathbed visions.

Lady Barrett delivered the baby of a woman named Doris on 12 January 1924. It was a difficult birth, and the mother died as a result. As Doris lay dying, she stared at a corner of the room, smiling peacefully, and said, "Oh, lovely, lovely." Lady Barrett asked her what was "lovely", and she replied, "What I see. Lovely brightness – wonderful beings." She then cried out, "Why, it's Father! Oh, he's so glad I'm coming; he is so glad." Lady Barrett then brought in the new-born child, and Doris looked at it and said, "Do you think I ought to stay for the baby's sake?" She then turned towards the corner of the room again and, speaking to nothingness, said, "I can't – I can't stay; if you could see what I do, you would know I can't stay. I am coming." Turning to Lady Barrett, she stared her in the eyes and said, "He has Vida with him." She then turned back to the corner of the room and said, "You do want me, Dad; I am coming." She died shortly afterwards.

What really amazed Sir William and Lady Barrett was the fact that Doris's sister Vida had died three weeks earlier. The Barretts had not told Doris this because of her own ill health and the impending birth. She had no way of knowing that Vida was dead, yet it appeared that she was somehow given knowledge of her existence in the afterlife. Sir William collected many such visions into a book, *Death-Bed Visions*. As a physician, he was well aware that many people suffer hallucinations under intense stress, but he noted that these visions were different. For example, the subject was more often than not clear and rational rather than hysterical. Also, if they were hallucinations, the mind would usually play a trick on the brain, making it think that it had seen something. In hallucinations, these sights will conform to a stereotype – the brain seeing what it thinks will be there. Yet Sir Barrett had cases of children who were surprised to see angels without wings, making him conclude that they were not suffering from mere hallucinations. Barrett's work fell on deaf ears for over thirty years. During this period, people were not interested in near-death experiences; they were more concerned with trying to communicate with those already departed. It was to be the late 1950s before anyone would follow up his work.

Parapsychologist Karlis Osis read Barrett's book and was inspired by it. He decided to undertake a full scientific investigation of near-death experiences, starting in 1959. Osis worked at the Parapsychology Foundation in New York at the time, and was able to talk with doctors and nurses about patients who had

had the experience. He conducted a survey over the period of a year, which seemed to support Barrett's hypothesis that near-death experiences were more than simple hallucinations. Osis concluded, using statistical methods, that the visions could not have been induced by drugs or fever, and that the visual nature of the experiences differed dramatically from the more auditory hallucinations common among the mentally ill. Near-death experiences, he found, were three times more likely to involve interaction with spirits of the dead than apparitions that were reported by people who were not dying.

In the 1970s, Osis followed up this simple survey with a far broader one, which he conducted for the American Society for Psychical Research. He teamed up with an Icelandic psychologist, Erlendur Haraldsson, and the two conducted comparative research on reports from America and India – two very culturally different nations.

Nearly two thousand people were interviewed to collect the data. The American and Indian experiences showed striking similarities, despite the cultural differences. Both saw apparitions whom they described as messengers or spirit guides from the next world, and the meeting with these beings was usually a joyful occasion. However, a significant number – nearly 30 per cent – said that they felt threatened by the spirit guide, that it seemed somehow evil. The main difference between the American and the Indian experience was that the Indians believed that the spirit guide was some form of religious figure, whereas the Americans believed it to be a dead friend or relative. At the end of the study, the two researchers concluded the following:

"We interpret these modest cultural differences according to our model: they seem to support the hypothesis that deathbed visions are, in part, based on extra-sensory perception of some form of external reality rather than having entirely subjective origins."

The study did not conclude that near-death experiences were proof of life after death. It did state, however, that near-death experiences hinted at the possibility of the immortality of the soul, but that there was insufficient evidence scientifically and categorically to state that this was fact.

The research into the field continued apace. One of the most famous researchers in the field was Dr Raymond Moody, who collected in the region of 150 accounts of NDEs, which he published in his book, *Life after Life*. In the book, Moody became the first to categorize the major elements which seem to be shared by the majority of NDEs (see page 76). Moody carefully defined a complete NDE as follows:

"A man is dying and, as he reaches the point of greatest physical distress, he hears himself pronounced dead by his doctor. He begins to hear an uncomfortable noise, a loud ringing or buzzing, and at the same time feels himself moving very rapidly through a long dark tunnel. After this, he suddenly finds himself outside of his own physical body, but still in the immediate physical environment, and he sees his own body from a distance, as though he is a spectator. He watches the resuscitation attempt from this unusual vantage point and is in a state of emotional upheaval.

"After a while, he collects himself and becomes more accustomed to his odd condition. He notices that he still has a 'body', but one of a very different nature and with very different powers from the physical body he left behind. Soon other things begin to happen. Others come to meet and to help him. He glimpses the spirits of relatives and friends who have already died, and a loving, warm spirit of a kind he has never encountered before – a being of light – appears before him. This being asks him a question, non-verbally, to make him evaluate his life and helps him along by showing him a panoramic, instantaneous playback of the major events of his life. At some point he finds himself approaching some sort of barrier or border, apparently representing the limit between earthly life and the next life. Yet, he finds that he must go back to the earth, that the time for his death has not yet come. At this point he resists, for by now he is taken up with his experiences in the afterlife and does not want to return. He is overwhelmed by intense feelings of joy, love and peace. Despite his attitude, though, he somehow reunites with his physical body and lives."

This is a very detailed description of the experience, and was intended by Moody to encompass all of the NDE phenomenon, although it was by no means experienced by all his subjects. Many would report parts of the phenomenon, but not all. One very common aspect is that the near-death experience may have produced the feeling of a beautiful place of golden tranquillity, which many assume is heaven. If this is indeed the case, then what of those who encounter the opposite. Would their experience suggest a glimpse of hell?

Angie Fenimore, author of *Beyond Darkness: My Near-Death Journey to Hell and Back*, faced exactly that question. She had her near-death experience just after she had attempted suicide, and she believes that it is possible that this affected the more usual feeling of euphoria associated with the phenomenon:

> *"Mine was initially extremely unpleasant because I had the feeling that committing suicide was the most serious action anyone could carry out."*

Angie saw her entire life laid out before her in great detail, a very common occurrence. She then went through a dark tunnel, and encountered a group of teenagers "entirely devoid of hope for themselves and didn't care at all what happened to me". She also met a group of people dressed in dirty, white robes whom she described as "wrapped up in their own torture". She claims that she was saved by a figure who suddenly appeared, who she is convinced was God, and who told her that life was supposed to be hard. The figure then showed her what life would be like for her children if she were to die. This finally convinced her to return to her body and continue with her life.

Another woman who experienced a vivid picture of darkness was former CID officer, Joyce Harvey. She is unusual because, unlike most people who have a near-death experience, hers began not with a sensation of floating above the body, but rather one of falling. She was in hospital, sitting next to her bed, reading, when she suddenly felt paralysed and a sensation of falling. She heard screams which sounded like children, and felt heat below her as though someone had opened an oven door beneath her feet. Then a sea of faces appeared below her, and scorching-hot hands reached out, clawing at her feet, and trying to pull her down the tunnel. She was absolutely terrified, more so than ever before in her life, and thought that if she were to die, she had to try to get into heaven. Just at that moment, she heard a voice calling her back, and she felt herself being sucked back into her physical body. A nurse was standing beside her, worried that she might have passed away, and curiously examining her legs. Her legs had mysteriously developed bruising, which Joyce could only assume had come from the creatures in the tunnel who had grabbed and pulled at her.

As research into near-death experiences continues, so does the debate over the central issue: the meaning of it all. It is no longer questioned that people honestly have the experience, but the crucial issues remain. Firstly, do NDEs prove psychic ability, the power of the mind and the existence of the soul? Secondly, do NDEs prove the existence of life after death, or is there a psychological or physiological explanation for them?

Theories for near-death experiences

The fact that nearly all those who have near-death experiences follow the same path towards a brilliant light would seem to be very strong evidence for suggesting that the whole thing is either a spiritual journey or a psychic power unleashed in the dying moments. However, this evidence – the shared experience of the phenomenon – is also used to support the theory that the NDE is not a spiritual voyage, but a function of the dying brain. Sceptics say that all brains, regardless of where they come from, die in the same way and that is why so many NDEs are the same. It is not because the dying person is being shown the joys of the afterlife, but because neurotransmitters in the brain are shutting down and creating the same illusions for all who are near death.

This approach, called the Dying Brain Theory, is not acceptable to the vast majority of people who have had a near-death experience. To reduce what was a profound and moving experience to nothing more than neurotransmitters malfunctioning seems to be a bit like reducing a Beethoven symphony to individual notes on a page. If the afterlife does not exist, why would the brain bother to produce such images in its death throes? If just an illusion, why do so many people return to their bodies having been told that it was not their time yet? Also, if the neurotransmitters have died, how do they re-form once a person has returned to the physical body? We all lose brain cells throughout our lives, and they never grow back.

The Hallucination Theory also tries to explain the phenomenon through brain activity. It is a widely accepted fact that long-distance runners can go through a pain barrier and find themselves running comfortably and with a feeling of elation, known as the "runner's high". This is caused by hormones released from the brain called endorphins which act on the central nervous system to suppress pain. Many scientists believe that a similar hormone is released into the system of dying patients, triggering a near-death experience. Ronald Siegel, a psychology professor in Los Angeles, claims to have reproduced NDEs in his laboratory by giving LSD to volunteers. His claims have been widely rejected by other researchers. Although drug-induced hallucinations may have some of the characteristics of a near-death experience, they are by no means the same thing. Drug-induced hallucinations merely distort reality, while the NDE is described as "hyper-reality".

Another possible explanation that has been the subject of investigation is the Lack of Oxygen Theory. This theory would have us believe that the whole experience is simply caused by a lack of oxygen, or excess of carbon dioxide, in the brain. However, the two experiences do not tally. Research has shown that the hallucinations produced by an oxygen-starved brain are chaotic, causing confusion and fear, compared with the tranquillity of the NDE. One researcher in the field, Dr Michael Sabom, has reports of patients who have had NDEs in hospital, and the medical equipment has shown that they have had more than sufficient oxygen in their brain to allow normal neural activity. Also, the vast majority of hallucinations caused by a lack of oxygen in the brain occur while the patient is conscious, whereas NDEs always occur while the patient is unconscious.

Another popular theory is the Memory of Birth Theory, which offers the opinion that the NDE is nothing to do with an augury of death, but is a memory of childbirth. A baby being born leaves the womb to travel towards a light. When it reaches the light, it is greeted with love and warmth. The "being of light" mentioned by many who have experienced a near-death experience is explained away as being the doctor or midwife. Those who argue the theory suggest that the feelings of peace and joy are simply a memory of the womb. This theory does, however, lack in many respects. Most reports of NDEs tell of a floating at high speed through the tunnel towards the light. This hardly tallies with a birth caused by a mother's contractions. Also, it goes no way towards explaining the meeting that most people have with people that they know, friends and relatives, who guide them on their journey.

The final theory seems to be the most plausible, and yet the one which is most rejected by the scientific community. The Afterlife Theory is the belief that the near-death experience shows a brief glimpse into the afterlife, the place where the soul goes when the physical body has died. Sceptics naturally refute this claim, on the grounds that there is no proof, but one leading researcher into the field suggests that the burden of proof should be on them. I agree with him. Until it is proven otherwise, the most likely explanation for the near-death experience is that it is a window into the next life. The researcher who placed the burden of proof on the sceptics is Dr Kenneth Ring, perhaps the most respected of all NDE researchers. As he put it:

> *"Any adequate neurological explanation would have to be capable of showing how the entire complex of phenomena associated with the core experience (that is, the out-of-body state, the golden light, the voice or presence, the appearance of deceased relatives, beautiful vistas, and so forth) would be expected to occur in subjectively authentic fashion as a consequence of specific neurological events triggered by the approach of death . . . I am tempted to argue that the burden of proof has now shifted to those who wish to explain near-death experiences this way."*

The search continues for an adequate explanation.

Until such time as science can explain near-death experiences in terms of neural activity, it can only be assumed that they are an insight into the next life, and that psychic ability is somehow enhanced at the point of death, enabling us to see what happens to us when we die.

Recovered memory and reincarnation

The belief in reincarnation – that a person's soul is reborn over and over again in another body or form – stretches far back into the pages of history. The doctrine appears in primitive religions such as those of tribes in India who believed that after death the soul took the form of an insect. The Bakongs of Borneo believed that their dead were reincarnated into the bearcats that massed around their raised coffins. The Kikuyu women of Kenya worship at a place they believe to be inhabited by their ancestral souls in the belief that they must be entered by an ancestral soul in order to become pregnant. According to Buddhist and Hindu doctrine, the soul is reborn in accordance with merits acquired during a previous lifetime. In other words, if you have lived a good life, then you will return in the next life in a peaceful and happy form. If you have led a bad life, then you could well return as a cactus or a lizard. The Buddhists believe that humans are made up of certain elements: body, sensation, perception, impulse, emotion and consciousness, which separate at death. When an individual dies, a new individual begins according to the quality of the previous life until, over a series of lives, perfection and eternal bliss is achieved.

The idea of reincarnation is not a new one to Western beliefs, although it has been shunned for many years, primarily because of Roman Catholic doctrines. Plato believed in reincarnation, seeing the soul as immortal, the number of souls as fixed, and reincarnation as an everyday part of life, death and regeneration. The Roman Catholic church, however, repudiated the idea as early as AD 553, when the Roman emperor Justinian condemned reincarnation as heresy. As a result, Western thinking today has some difficulty in identifying with the idea of reincarnation. It was again denounced as heresy by the Roman Catholic church in 1917. But the weight of evidence is mounting in favour of the principle, regardless of the thinking of the Roman Catholic church. Just as near-death experiences offer insight into the possibility of an afterlife, so too does regressive hypnosis into past lives. If there are past lives, then there must surely also be future ones?

The German philosopher Arthur Schopenhauer said,

> *"Were an Asiatic to ask me for a definition of Europe, I should be forced to answer him: 'It is that part of the world which is haunted by the incredible delusion that man was created out of nothing. And that his present birth is his first entrance into life.'"*

Nevertheless, the belief in reincarnation in the Western world is growing. The British newspaper, the *Daily Mail*, held a survey in 1998 which found that 25 per cent of all those surveyed believed in reincarnation.

The primary case for reincarnation lies with

hypnotic regression. People are regressed back to such a point that they begin to talk about their experiences in a past life. The power of hypnosis is discussed in greater detail in Chapter 7. The main problem with hypnotic regression is that it may unwittingly be accessing other psychic areas of the mind such as telepathy, clairvoyance, etc. Other studies into reincarnation have been undertaken, however, which do not involve hypnosis. Probably the most significant body of work collected in the field is that of Dr Ian Stevenson, a parapsychologist at the University of Virginia. Stevenson believes that hypnotic regression is not useful in the study of reincarnation, and has analysed over 2,500 cases using alternative methods. Stevenson's work centres mainly on children who have reported an earlier, untimely death. His subjects often show physical features which are suggestive of their previous lives and deaths. His research covers the globe, including many societies where a belief in reincarnation is the norm, and is actively celebrated.

One of Stevenson's investigations centred on Gopal Gupta, who was born in Delhi, India, in 1956. At a very young age, Gopal began acting in a way which was out of character for his social class. The caste system is very strong in India, and from a very early age people are taught to remain within their level of society and act accordingly. When asked to pick up a glass of water, he refused to do so, claiming that he was a sharma (a member of India's highest caste, the Brahmins). He went on to explain that he had once owned a company called Sukh Shancharak, had lived in the city of Mathura, and that he had been murdered by one of his brothers in his previous life. When he was nine, Gopal was taken on a trip to Mathura by his father. The two of them sought out the company, Sukh Shancharak, and found out, to their amazement, that one of the owners had been shot and killed by his brother in 1948.

Many people have contended that this information could have been given to Gopal through some other psychic ability – perhaps he was receiving a message from the dead. Whether this is true, or Gopal was in fact the reincarnation of the murdered sharma, can never be proved, but either way some part of that man appears to have lived on after death in order for the information to be passed on. As Gopal matured into adulthood, he became absorbed into his caste and, as it were, gave up the ghost of his past life. This seems to be the case with the majority of Stevenson's cases, which is why his study centres on children. One case, however, in which the subject's memories did not fade with the approach of adulthood, is the case of Swarnlata.

Swarnlata Mishra was born in 1948 in Pradesh, India, to a well-educated and prosperous family. When she was only three years old and travelling with her father past the town of Katni, more than 100 miles from her home, she suddenly pointed and asked the driver to turn down a road to "my house". She went on to say that they would get a better cup of tea there than they would on the road. Soon after this incident, she started to relate more details about her previous existence, all of which were written down by her father. Some of the information she passed on was incredibly specific. She said her name was Biya Pathak, and that she had two sons. Her house was white with black doors and iron bars, and the floor was made of stone slabs. Her house was in Zhurkutia, a district of Katni, behind which was a school for girls, and in front of which was a railway line. She claimed to have died from a "pain in her throat", having been treated for her illness by Dr Bhabrat in Jabalpur.

When she was ten years old, Swarnlata's story came to the attention of Professor Sri Banerjee, an Indian researcher of the paranormal, and a colleague of Dr Stevenson. Banerjee took the notes that her father had painstakingly written down over the years, and travelled to Katni to see how accurate her descriptions were. He found the house, using only the descriptions that Swarnlata had given, and found that it belonged to the Pathak family. One hundred yards to the rear of the house was a girls' school, and about the same distance away from the front of the house was a railway line. Banerjee interviewed the Pathak family, and found out that their mother, Biya Pathak had died in 1939, leaving behind a grieving husband and two young sons. The Pathaks had never heard of the Mishra family.

Naturally, the Pathaks were intrigued by what Dr Banerjee had to tell them about the experiences of Swarnlata, and in 1959 Biya's widower, son and eldest brother travelled to the town of Chatarpur, where Swarnlata lived at the time, to test her recovered memory. They kept their identities secret to everyone in the town, and asked nine other townsfolk to accompany them to Swarnlata's house, where they arrived unannounced. Swarnlata immediately recognized her brother and called him "Babu", which was Biya's nickname for him. She then went round the room, looking at each man in turn. Some were complete strangers to her, and some were people she knew from the town. Then she came to Biya's widower. She lowered her eyes and spoke his name. She then went on correctly to identify Murli, her son from her previous life, but Murli decided to test her to the limit. For almost twenty-four hours, he insisted that he was not Murli, but someone else, but Swarnlata would have none of it. The man in front of her was most definitely her son.

A few weeks later, Swarnlata's father took her to the Pathaks' home in Katni. Upon arriving, she immediately pointed out the changes that had been made to the house. She correctly identified both Biya's room, and the room in which she had died. She identified her brothers, the wife of the younger brother, the son of the second brother and other relations. She was then led into a room full of strangers, and was asked to identify people whom she recognized. She correctly picked out her husband's cousin, the wife of Biya's brother-in-law and a midwife. Murli presented her with another test, by introducing her to a man whom he said was his friend, Bhola. Swarnlata, however, insisted that it was Biya's second son, Naresh, and she was correct. Another member of the family also tried to trick her by stating that Biya had lost her teeth. Swarnlata replied that this was a lie, and that she had only had gold fillings in her front teeth, another truth which amazed the family. What was even more amazing was that Swarnlata's knowledge of the family ended at the time of Biya's death. She knew nothing about the Pathak family that had happened since 1939.

In the following years, Swarnlata visited the Pathak family regularly. Dr Stevenson investigated the case in 1961, when he witnessed one of these visits, and he observed that the Pathak family had taken Swarnlata into the fold, fully accepting her as Biya reborn. Swarnlata and the Pathak brothers observed the Hindu custom of Rakhi, in which brothers and sisters renew their devotion to each other every year by exchanging gifts. The brothers were greatly distressed and angry one year when Swarnlata missed the ceremony – they believed that because she had lived with them for forty years, and with her "new" family for only ten years, they had the greater claim over her. As evidence of how strongly the Pathaks believed that Swarnlata was their matriarch, they admitted that they had changed their views on reincarnation (previously, because of their wealth and status, they had emulated Western ideologies and had not believed in reincarnation before this all happened). Swarnlata's father also accepted her claim about her past life, and when, years later, she came to marry, he consulted with the Pathaks about the choice of a husband for her.

This case illustrates what a profound experience a past life memory can bring about. The two families are still united in their belief that Swarnlata is the reincarnation of Biya, and with all the evidence before them, who can blame them? Their lives are more complete because of the experience, but the intrusive nature of some of the cases researched by Dr Stevenson can show a darker side to the phenomenon.

The case of another Indian boy, Ravi Shankar, encapsulates many of the recurrent elements found in Stevenson's studies, but has one extra feature which marks it out as special. In 1953, when Ravi was two, he began to talk to his parents about a former life in a neighbouring district, and described several of his previous-life toys – a ball on an elastic string, a toy pistol and a wooden elephant. He also mentioned that he kept a ring in a desk at his former house. He called his previous father by name, and claimed that he was a barber. Disturbingly, he then went on to tell his parents that he had been murdered in his previous life, and even identified his murderers by name. Just before he died, he had been eating guavas, and his murderers had killed him by cutting his throat.

Two years later, when Ravi was four, a man who had heard stories of Ravi's tales of a previous life visited his family. He told Ravi's parents that his own six-year-old son had been killed six months before Ravi's birth in the exact manner Ravi described. The names and occupations of the men whom Ravi claimed killed him exactly matched those of two men related to the victim. As a result of the boy's death, they had gained a large inheritance. One of the two men had previously confessed to the murder, but then recanted his confession, and was not brought to trial due to lack of evidence.

Dr Stevenson soon heard of the story and in 1964, when Ravi was thirteen, he undertook an investigation into the case. He discovered that a teacher had taken detailed notes on Ravi's claims when he was five, and Stevenson was able to confirm twenty-six separate statements from it as fact, including all the toys that Ravi had mentioned, and the ring in the desk. It also turned out that the victim of the murder had been eating guavas immediately prior to his death. Stevenson found out that Ravi had had a phobia of knives and razors since very early in life, and that he was terribly afraid to go to the area where the murder had been committed. But what really amazed Stevenson was the unusual birthmark that Ravi had, a strange scar on his neck which his mother had first noticed when he was only three months old. The "birthmark" was two inches long and a quarter of an inch wide. Stevenson described it as having "the stippled quality of a scar. It looked much like an old scar of a healed knife wound". Had Ravi brought the wound with him from a previous life? It does indeed seem a little too bizarre simply to be shrugged off as coincidence.

Stevenson has countless cases like it to back up the evidence from Ravi. Nevertheless, he is not without his critics, as is so often the case when dealing with the paranormal. Even his critics, however, acknowledge that Stevenson employs exceptionally high standards in all his investigations, but they do point out areas that they believe could allow fraudulent stories to pass through the net. Ian Wilson claims that in many of Stevenson's case histories, including Ravi Shankar, the supposedly reborn child or its family may have learned more about the previous life from other people than they have told Stevenson. He also notes that some poor Indian families (as in the case of Swarnlata above) might just claim a higher-caste previous life for their children in the hope of acquiring financial and social advantages. Many critics also claim that Stevenson is so obsessed with reincarnation as an explanation for the cases he has studied, that he would dismiss any other possible explanation.

Stevenson's defenders, however, point out that Stevenson himself provides most of the ammunition for his critics in his scrupulous case studies and cautious arguments. He meticulously examines all sides of every case that he investigates before reaching the conclusion that reincarnation is a possible explanation for them. He has never said that his studies categorically prove the case for reincarnation, only that no normal explanation comfortably fits the facts. In an article on his work, published in the *Journal of the American Medical Association* in 1975, the writer stated that Stevenson "had collected cases in which the evidence is difficult to explain on any other grounds besides reincarnation".

Reincarnation is considered to be fact by so many people throughout the world, but it is only one explanation for what happens to us after we die, and only one explanation for what happens to our spirit after it leaves the physical body. Could it be the case that not all of us are reincarnations of previous lives – that some of us are on our first visit – while others have lived many times before? Perhaps those who believe that they have had previous lives are simply profoundly strong channellers of spirits, with incredible psychic abilities and able to receive information from the dead. Perhaps we will never know, but the next chapter examines the birth of various schools of thought that have endeavoured to answer these and many other psychic-related issues. It may happen that one or more of these societies will finally come up with the answers to the eternal questions circling the secrets of the mind and the soul.

Psychic art

Many mediums claim that they have the ability to contact the spirits of the deceased. A select few sensitives claim that they have contacted famous people from all walks of life, including renowned artists, painters and composers. Some of these great spirits, it seems, were not content with what they had achieved while alive, and appear to be using mediums to continue their work.

A London housewife, Rosemary Brown, claims to be a channeller for several of the great composers, including Beethoven, Brahms, Debussy, Chopin, Schubert and Stravinsky. When she was a child, she had visions of an elderly man who repeatedly told her that he and other great composers would teach her their wonderful music. It was only many years later that she saw a picture of Franz Lizst and recognized him as her spectral friend. In 1964, she claims, she was first contacted by Beethoven and other great composers, and began to channel their unfinished symphonies. The pieces received by her are complete compositions, mainly for the piano, but sometimes for a full orchestra. Mrs Brown says that the music is already composed when it is given to her; the composers simply dictate it to her as fast as she can scribble it down. Observers who have watched Mrs Brown in action are amazed at the speed at which she writes the music down, and slightly awed by the standard of the music, which goes far beyond her own knowledge, for she has never been musically trained. During the writing sessions, Mrs Brown chats with her spiritual guests as she writes, and transcribes the work far faster than most musicians could possibly compose.

But are these new compositions recognizably the works of the great composers? Concert pianist Hephzibah Menuhin said:

> *"I look at these manuscripts with immense respect. Each piece is distinctly in the composer's style."*

British composer Richard Rodney Bennett had the following to say when he looked at Mrs Brown's manuscripts:

"A lot of people can improvise, but you couldn't fake music like this without years of training. I couldn't have faked some of the Beethoven myself."

Mrs Brown has also, so she says, been contacted by dead artists, poets, playwrights, scientists and philosophers. Vincent van Gogh has communicated his works through her, and Einstein apparently explains difficult scientific theory to her. And she is not alone in her ability to channel the great artists of the world.

British concert pianist, John Lill, also claims inspiration from the dead composers for his piano playing. When he was practising in the Moscow Conservatoire for the Tchaikovsky Piano Competition, he became aware of a figure watching him who was wearing archaic clothing. He believes that this figure was in fact the spirit of Beethoven, with whom he claims to have held many conversations ever since that first "meeting". Handel is apparently channelled through medium Clifford Enticknap. Mr Enticknap explains that Handel was his music tutor in a previous life, and that their relationship as master and student dates back to a former incarnation when the two of them lived in Atlantis! Handel allegedly communicated a four-and-a-half-hour-long oratorio entitled Beyond the Veil to Enticknap, and a seventy-three-minute excerpt of this has now been recorded by the London Symphony Orchestra and the Handelian Foundation Choir. It is available on tape through the Handelian Foundation, who claim that it is proof that Handel's abilities as a composer have survived death.

Great literary geniuses are also said to have continued their work beyond the grave. In 1947, Hester Dowden, a medium, claimed that she had channelled the works of great writers from centuries ago. Dowden's claim was made more famous because she cast doubt on the works of Shakespeare – asserting that they were in fact the work of three authors, William Shakespeare, Francis Bacon and Lord Oxford, all of whom she claimed to have channelled. If Mrs Dowden is to be believed, then the Shakespearean plays were principally written by Shakespeare and Lord Oxford, while Bacon acted as a stern script editor. Shakespeare created all the strong characters, while Lord Oxford provided the lyrical and romantic passages, and also wrote the majority of the sonnets. Mrs Dowden channelled three new sonnets from Lord Oxford, all in the Shakespearean style.

In truth, the majority of psychic and paranormal researchers dismiss the claims of these mediums as nonsense, despite the extraordinary music and literature that they write down. If they are not channelling the spirits of the great composers and authors, though, where is all this great music and literature coming from? It certainly doesn't come from the conscious mind of Mrs Brown, for she knows nothing about music, yet she writes the notes down perfectly. One school of thought believes that our deeper inspirations come from the "Akashic records", a universal consciousness that encompasses all human thought. In certain states of mind, particularly in trance-like states, this hidden knowledge becomes available to the conscious mind. To the mediums themselves, it is simple. The ability of these people to channel music and literature in this way is yet another piece of evidence to support the theory that death is simply a transition from this life to the next.

Science and Spiritualism

....

The birth of Spiritualism

Spiritualism is the belief, or practices based upon the belief, that departed souls can communicate with humans, usually through a medium, either in dreams or trances. Spiritualists believe in the "spirit", the essential part of a human being which lives on after the death of the body. The attempt to communicate with the spirit world has concerned humankind since time immemorial, yet Spiritualist practices, although wide-spread throughout the world, were virtually unknown in Western society until March 1848, the year which most researchers agree to mark the birth of Spiritualism.

The beginnings of the belief can be traced back to the strange happenings reported at the house of a farmer named Fox in the small town of Hydesville in New York state. Margaretta and Catherine Fox, who became known to the world as Maggie and Kate, received a very staid, Methodist upbringing. Their father had no interest in spiritual matters – the only spirits that John Fox knew were the bottled variety, and he had banned those from their household.

One night, in March 1848, strange noises were heard in the house, loud booms which actually made the

The famous Fox sisters – who founded the Spiritual movement on a hoax.

structure shudder. The Fox family leapt out of bed and searched the house for what they thought must have been an intruder. They found nothing, but the noises continued for over a week. On the last day of March, the Fox family retired to bed, worn out by nights of continual noise. The two sisters, thoroughly frightened, had moved into their parents' bedroom. As the family finally drifted off to sleep, the noises started once more, waking them all up in an instant. Kate Fox had had enough of sleepless nights, and on this occasion she attempted to confront the source of the mysterious banging. She clicked her fingers, and asked the "noise" to respond. To the utter amazement of her family, the noise did indeed respond. Mrs Fox then asked it to bang ten times, which it duly did. She then asked it to tap out the ages of her six children; again, it obliged, accurately. Over the next few weeks, the family developed a sophisticated rapping system to communicate with the "spirit". Silence on the part of the spirit indicated a "no", and one rap indicated a "yes". They then developed different raps for each letter of the alphabet. The spirit, using this system, identified itself as the ghost of a peddler who had been robbed and killed in their house by a former resident, and he claimed that his body was buried in the basement. During an excavation of their basement floor, the Fox family later uncovered human teeth, hair and bones.

News of the strange phenomenon soon spread through the small community and beyond, and the press got hold of the story. A reporter by the name of E. E. Lewis visited the family and interviewed them, and their neighbours, about their paranormal experiences. He published a pamphlet entitled *A Report of*

*the Mysterious Noises Heard in the House of Mr John
D. Fox*, which has become known as the very first
Spiritualist publication. The press loved the story, but
even so, the Fox family's experiences would have
been seen as an isolated incident, were it not for
Maggie and Kate's older sister, Mrs Leah Fox Fish.

Mrs Fish was the oldest of the Fox children, lived in
Rochester, New York, some thirty miles from
Hydesville, and had a daughter of Maggie's age. Her
husband had left her, leaving her to fend for herself
and their child, and she had managed to do so
successfully by teaching music. Leah got hold of a
copy of *A Report of the Mysterious Noises Heard in the
House of Mr John D. Fox*, and saw dollar signs before
her eyes. Leah took Maggie and Kate on tour, unwittingly unleashing a new movement upon the world –
the Spiritualist movement. Maggie and Kate
performed in séance rooms and university lecture
theatres, and eventually attracted the backing of the
famous P. T. Barnum, who took them to New York
and made them international stars. Spiritualism had
now become a circus show, but its overall development was to extend far more widely than anyone
could have predicted from such humble beginnings.

Spiritualism spread like wildfire after the events in
Hydesville and the promotion of the Fox sisters to
international fame. Five years after the first tappings
were heard, there were an estimated 30,000 mediums
in America alone. By the end of the 1850s, much to
the consternation of the burgeoning scientific movement, the public had in general accepted that the
human spirit survives death, and that certain gifted
people were able to communicate with those who
had passed on. Psychic powers became the great

topic of discussion in Victorian parlours, and the Spiritualist movement mutated from a circus show into a more mature and mysterious art form.

When Spiritualism first spread to Europe, its most popular manifestation was table turning. This occurred usually during a séance, when the medium would use his or her power apparently to overturn a table without touching it – the forerunner of psychokinesis. It soon became the biggest source of amazement and amusement for the chattering classes, but others took it very seriously indeed. Abraham Lincoln was allegedly prompted to issue the Emancipation Proclamation as a result of conversations with spirits through a well-known medium; Queen Victoria is rumoured to have tried to contact Prince Albert after his death through similar means.

By 1855, Spiritualism had over two million followers. Amazing stories of psychic powers circulated the globe at fever pitch. Spiritualism finally knew that it had arrived when it became publicly condemned by leaders of organized religions, who attempted to get laws passed banning the movement. Many mediums became ostracized by friends and family, and investigators began looking into and exposing the vast number of fraudulent mediums that were operating in America and the United Kingdom.

The biggest blow for the Spiritualist movement came with a revelation from one of its "founders" in 1888, forty years after its conception. In a public appearance in New York, Maggie Fox, who had by now converted to Catholicism, stated that Spiritualism was both evil and a fraud, and that she and Kate had been faking phenomena all the years they had been in practice. Furthermore, the events at Hydesville in 1848 were revealed to be an elaborate hoax. When Leah had gone to visit her sisters all those years ago, they told her how the "paranormal" tappings had actually happened. Maggie and Kate had begun very simply by tying an apple to a string and, while lying in bed, bobbing it up and down to bump against the floor, purely to play a joke on their mother. Once the crowds started to flock to their house, they found that the apple trick would be too difficult to hide, so they came up with something much more cunning. On 21 October 1888, Maggie appeared before an audience of 2000 to demonstrate how she had produced the spirit-rapping for forty years. In her stockinged feet, on a small platform, she produced rapping noises by cracking her toe joints which could be heard throughout the theatre. This, she claimed, was how she and her sister had fooled the world for nearly half a century.

It appeared that the entire Spiritualist movement had been founded on a fraud, the result of a girlish prank which got out of hand. But the movement had far outgrown its creators, and Spiritualists were outraged at the Fox sisters' allegations. Many simply refused to believe what they were saying. The president of the First Spiritualist Society of New York said at the time:

> *"The idea of claiming that unseen 'rappings' can be produced with joints of the feet! If she says this, even with regard to her own manifestations, she lies! I and many other men of truth and position have witnessed the manifestations of herself and her sisters many times under circumstances in*

*which it was absolutely impossible for there to
have been the least fraud."*

In Spiritualist terms, the revelation was a bit like
Jesus Christ informing Christians that God does not
exist. The creator of the fictional detective Sherlock
Holmes, Sir Arthur Conan Doyle, was a firm believer
in all things paranormal, and a devout Spiritualist.
When he heard Maggie's admission, he responded:

*"Nothing that she could say in that regard would
in the least change my opinion, nor it would that
of anyone else who had become profoundly
convinced that there is an occult influence
connecting us with an invisible world."*

Conan Doyle became famous for his interest in the
spirit world and all things paranormal. He was also
known to believe in fairies, and was convinced that
he had photographs of them to prove it. One man,
G. K. Chesterton, said of Conan Doyle, ". . . it has long
seemed to me that Sir Arthur's mentality is much
more that of Watson that it is of Holmes".

The Society for Psychical Research

For all its rather too obvious flaws, the Spiritualist
movement woke people up to the possibilities of the
mind's powers. The Society for Psychical Research
was founded in 1882 in London by Sir William Barrett
and Edmund Dawson Rogers because of their inter-
ests in Spiritualism, and their desire for the development of an organization to research related

phenomena, namely ghosts, trance states, telepathy, clairvoyance and other extra-sensory powers. The initial organization was composed mainly of enthusiastic Spiritualists, but a group within the society soon emerged as an experienced team of paranormal investigators.

Six research committees were set up within the Society for Psychical Research, and each one was given a remit to study a particular aspect of spiritualistic and psychical phenomena. The six committees were as follows:

1. Thought transference (later renamed "telepathy")
2. Mesmerism, hypnotism, clairvoyance and related phenomena
3. "Sensitives" and "mediums", being people with the ability to communicate with the spirits of the deceased
4. Apparitions of all types
5. Levitations, materializations and other physical phenomena associated with séances
6. The collection and collation of data on the history of the above five subjects.

Inadvertently then, the Fox sisters had started a movement which would, over the years, become increasingly involved in the scientific study of the paranormal on a global scale. The founders of the Society for Psychical Research have even, allegedly, continued in their quest to prove the existence of psychic powers from beyond the grave.

For thirty years following his death in 1901, Frederick Myers, one of the founders of the SPR, passed on correspondences to mediums all over the world, in one of the most controversial cases in the history of psychic investigation. The SPR collected over 2000 "automatic scripts" which they believe came from Myers and other deceased members of the society through the mediumship of several ladies. If the story is to be believed, then Myers and his colleagues wished to prove that there was communication between the living and the dead – in effect, they had worked out a system which would prove the existence of an afterlife as fact. After their deaths, Myers et al contacted mediums from all over the world and channelled writings through them. Each individual script was utterly meaningless, but when brought together as a whole they would make sense.

The Society for Psychical Research's catalogue of cross-correspondences remains the most lengthy and complex in the history of psychical research. Shortly after Myers's death, messages said to be from him began appearing in "automatic writing" from five women connected with the SPR. They were: Margaret Verrall, a classics scholar and wife of a classics professor at Cambridge; her daughter, Helen, also a classics scholar; Alice Kipling Fleming, the sister of author Rudyard Kipling and wife of a British officer living in India; Winifred Coombe-Tenant, a very well-known and respected lady who had once been a representative to the League of Nations; and Leonora Piper, a professional medium. Some of these women knew each other, some never met in their lifetimes.

The cross-correspondences continued for over thirty years, and during this time, seven more mediums channelled messages in addition to the five mentioned above, and four more spirits in addition to

Myers offered their contributions. The scripts dictated by the spirits were received by the women through a process of automatic writing, whereby the receiver would fall into a trance, and write down what was "given" to them by the spirit. They had no idea that they were writing at the time, and would come out of their trance to find the script in front of them. The scripts themselves were fragmentary and extremely obscure, often referring to ancient little-known books in Latin and Greek. They were most often signed either "Myers" or "Gurney" (Edmund Gurney, another founder of the SPR, who died in 1888), and taken on an individual basis, they seemed totally meaningless. It was some time before anyone noticed that they seemed to be part of some large, elaborate puzzle, and investigators started to take an interest.

Alice Kipling Fleming had been producing such automatic scripts in India for some time before she became aware that mediums elsewhere in the world were also receiving these bizarre messages. One script instructed her to send it to an address in Cambridge – 5 Selwyn Gardens – a city that she had never visited. She duly sent a letter to that address, and enclosed the automatic script. The person who lived at the address was Margaret Verrall, who also had been receiving messages from Myers and, on receiving a cross-correspondence, the investigation began. Eventually, all the cross-correspondences were sent to the SPR, where investigators painstakingly pieced them together. It proved to be very hard work, for the writings were disjointed and relied very heavily on symbolism – it seemed as though the dead were deliberately trying to be obscure in order to force a proper investigation into the phenomenon.

In life, Myers had been a student and admirer of ancient Rome, and it appeared that his interest continued in death. On 2 March 1906, he channelled a script to Margaret Verrall containing a line of verse in Latin from Virgil's *Aeneid*, a classical epic poem about the Trojan Wars and the founding of Rome. In that script, and two subsequent ones written two days later, he made references to several Roman emperors and other figures important to the history of Christianized Rome. Two days after Mrs Verrall received these scripts, Mrs Kipling Fleming, who was in India at the time, produced a script on a similar theme. It included the words: "Ave Roma immortalis. [Hail immortal Rome.] How could I make it any clearer without giving her the clue?" This case was the beginning of a new theme in the cross-correspondences in which Myers predicted a new world order based on the Roman model. The writings went on to suggest that a new race, the "children of the spirit" would suffer through world wars and other disasters in order to bring about a new Utopian world.

This proved to be a major theme in the writings, but interwoven were smaller, more intimate messages, including a very famous love story. The case concerned two wealthy, aristocratic British families, the Balfours and the Lyttletons. Arthur Balfour was one of eight children, and Mary Lyttleton one of twelve. Their families moved in the same social circles, and they were good friends. Arthur met Mary in 1871 at a Christmas ball held by the Prime Minister, William Gladstone. The two privileged young people fell in love, and shared a deepening friendship over the next four years. Arthur finally

professed his love to Mary in 1875, but shortly afterwards, she contracted typhoid. She told Arthur that
his love was reciprocated, though it was all too late.
She died on the Palm Sunday of that year. Balfour was
distraught by Mary's death, and although he went on
to have a very successful career, he never married.
Every year until his death he spent Palm Sunday
alone with Mary's sister.

Within the cross-correspondences, there are a great
many suggestions that Mary's spirit survived, and
that it tried unsuccessfully over the years to contact
Arthur Balfour to communicate Mary's continuing
love for him. The scripts came in from four different
receivers, none of whom would have known the story
of the love affair. In fact, hardly anyone outside the
Balfour and Lyttleton households would have known
about it. The "Palm Sunday scripts" were kept a
secret for many years, the SPR eventually
bequeathing them to Balfour's niece, who decided to
have them published in 1960.

Again though, the references in the scripts were
obscure and needed much translating. There were
references to the Palm Maiden, the Blessed Damozel,
Berenice and May Blossom. Palm Sunday was the day
of her death; the Blessed Damozel was the subject of
a poem by Dante Gabriel Rossetti in which a dead
maiden waits in heaven for her lover to join her;
Berenice was famous for sacrificing her beautiful hair;
May Blossom was Mary Lyttleton's family nickname.
The clues continued to mount up, but it was not until
1916 that Arthur Balfour agreed to sit with Mrs
Coombe-Tenant, one of the receivers. He immediately recognized clues that nobody else but he could
decipher. There were references in the correspond-

ences to a candle and a candlestick, to a metal box, and to purple periwinkle and a lock of hair. Arthur's most treasured photograph of Mary shows her holding a candle in a candlestick. But what really amazed Arthur was the reference to the metal box, which he had kept a secret from everyone for nearly forty years. Balfour had kept a silver box in his room ever since Mary's death; within it were the purple flower of a periwinkle, and a lock of Mary's hair.

The writings continued to pour in until, in 1932, they suddenly stopped. Whether the dead Frederick Myers was the true source of these automatic writings remains an unanswered question to most people who have studied the phenomenon. The fact remains that Myers left a much larger legacy – the Society for Psychical Research itself. The society is now a much respected research foundation which uses scientific methods to investigate fully psychical phenomena on a global scale. Since its inception, it has promoted research into the field from a variety of sources, creating a growing bank of knowledge on the subject area which may, one day, provide sufficient evidence to prove the existence of psychic powers.

Synchronicity and the collective unconscious

Running concurrently with the growth of the Spiritualist movement was the growth of the psychology movement. Sigmund Freud, now considered to be the Father of Psychology, undertook extensive research into the field of dreams. He once stated that the goal of therapy was to make the unconscious

conscious. Nevertheless, he made the unconscious sound extremely unpleasant – a cauldron of seething desires, a bottomless pit of perverse and incestuous cravings. A colleague of his, Carl Jung, was to make the exploration of this "inner space" his life's work.

Jung himself was prone to very vivid dreams, which sometimes appeared prophetic. In the autumn of 1913, he had a vision of a monstrous flood engulfing most of Europe. He saw thousands of people drowning, and civilization crumbling. Then the waters turned into blood. This vision was followed over a series of weeks by dreams of eternal winters and rivers of blood. The following year saw the outbreak of World War I, and Jung felt that there had been a connection, somehow, between himself as an individual and humanity in general that could not be explained away. From that point in time until 1928, Jung went through a period of self-exploration. He carefully recorded his dreams, fantasies and visions, and found that his experiences tended to form themselves into persons, beginning with a wise old man and his companion, a little girl. The wise old man evolved, over a number of dreams, into a sort of spiritual guru, and the little girl became the feminine soul, who served as his main medium of communication with the deeper aspects of his unconscious.

Jung dreamed a great deal about the dead, the land of the dead and the rising of the dead. To him, these represented the unconscious itself – not the personal unconscious of a single individual, but the collective unconscious of humanity itself. The idea of a collective unconscious became a major theory in psychology and now, parapsychology. The collective unconscious is believed to be an area of the psyche

Carl Jung, the man behind the theories of the collective
unconscious and synchronicity.

that contains all the dead, not just our own personal ghosts, a form of "psychic inheritance". It is the reservoir of our experiences as a species, a knowledge that we are all born with and yet we can never be directly conscious of. Jung believed that we often receive messages from the collective unconscious in the form of dreams, or in the trance-like states of mediums. The collective unconscious allows us to access a pool of knowledge from the moment we are born. It enables a baby to know first that it wants food, and second how to get it – by screaming for its mother's attention. It influences all our experiences and behaviours, most especially the emotional ones. There are some experiences that show the effects of the collective unconscious more clearly than others – the experience of love at first sight, the feeling of déjà vu and the immediate recognition of certain symbols which have never been explained to us.

Perhaps the best evidence in support of the collective unconscious is the phenomenon of the near-death experience (see Chapter 5). People from all over the world, regardless of culture or life-experience, who have undergone a near-death experience almost always report the same events. They speak of leaving their bodies, seeing their bodies and the events surrounding them clearly, of being pulled through a tunnel towards a brilliant light, of meeting deceased friends and relatives or religious figures who act as spirit guides, and finally of returning to their bodies. Perhaps we are all pre-programmed to experience death in this way. Or perhaps when we die, we become a part of the collective unconscious itself. If so, then are mediums who allegedly channel messages from the spirit world simply more in tune with the collective unconscious, closer somehow to that accumulation of universal experience to which we somehow all have access?

Jung also endeavoured to explain why coincidences are more than just random events. "Coincidence" is a word often used by sceptics to refute the claims of anyone who has had a paranormal experience. But for Jung, calling an event a "coincidence" did not automatically shut the door on any further examination of the facts. Coincidences happen, we all know that that is a fact. Furthermore, coincidences often seem to have a meaning to the participants. Jung pointed out that there can be very few people who have not at some point in their lives had some experience that they would describe as a "meaningful coincidence". Most of us would agree that there is something more to them than simple chance – consider the case described in Chapter 8 about the coincidences surrounding the fictional ship the *Titan* and the horrible reality of the *Titanic*. In his essay on synchronicity, Jung explored the field of coincidence. He stated that the natural laws by which we live are based on the principle of *causality* – if this thing happens, that thing will follow it. But Jung goes on to say that there are facts that the principle of causality *cannot* explain – ESP, verified cases of precognition or clairvoyance, and meaningful coincidences. Jung was at pains to emphasize what he saw as the true significance of many synchronistic events. He offered many examples from his own experience, including the case of a patient who was relating a dream to him. She was telling Jung of her dream that involved a golden scarab – a particularly potent symbol of regeneration, especially in ancient Egypt. As she spoke, an insect flew in through the window and, to his amazement, Jung identified it as a rose scarab, the closest thing to a golden scarab that can be found in mainland Europe. The patient made a full recovery – a regeneration, and Jung did not fail to see the significance of the event.

But isolated events such as this, however amazing they may appear, were insufficient for Jung, and he sought to build a much larger database of material. He chose to examine a body of traditional processes where the idea of synchronicity is taken for granted – the forms of divination that are essentially designed to interpret the meanings of coincidence. Jung looked at evidence from philosophies all over the world and, from his observations, drew some conclusions about synchronicity and the crucial role that the human psyche plays in it. Coincidences may be purely random events, but as soon as they seem to carry some symbolic meaning, they cease to be random as far as the person involved is concerned. Jung even considered the idea that the psyche can somehow cause coincidences to happen – a true psychic phenomenon. In the face of a meaningful coincidence, Jung says, we can respond to it in one of three ways. We can call it "mere random chance" and think nothing more of it; we can call it magic, or telepathy or ESP; or we can consider the existence of a principle of acausality, a connecting principle governing chains of events in stark contrast to our normal perception of things, causality.

Jung's research, unfortunately, cannot be quantified or proven. His ideas were just that – ideas, but Jung's idea of synchronicity does, at the very least, indicate vast frontiers that await exploration. His ideas led to a flurry of scientific investigation into unexplainable phenomena that are now classed as the paranormal, and his theory of the collective unconscious is one that is still supported by many practitioners. Perhaps the spirit world is in fact just in our minds, quite literally.

Altered States

• •

A certain stigma?

The curious phenomenon of stigmata has been researched for centuries. Over the past 775 years, over 300 people have reported this strange and often painful condition. They have displayed wounds on their bodies, particularly the hands and feet, which they fully believe represent the wounds which Christ suffered during his crucifixion. But how did these wounds appear? Were the recipients visited by Christ himself, or was it the strength of their beliefs which induced the stigmata? If the latter, then one must ask how much can a mind, convinced of a reality, directly affect the body? Perhaps stigmata are proof of the mind's phenomenal power to affect the physical body.

The very first piece of evidence appeared in 1224, when St Francis of Assisi was stigmatized while on a spiritual retreat in Italy. He was praying outside a cave when he saw a winged angel in the sky, and then fell into a trance-like state. The stigmata apparently appeared on him as he struggled up from the ground. Thomas de Celano, St Francis's biographer, gave a very detailed description of the stigmata, although his account was written three years after the saint's death:

"His hands and feet seemed pierced in the midst by nails, the heads of the nails appearing in the inner part of the hands and in the upper part of the feet, and their points over against them . . . Moreover his right side, as if it had been pierced by a lance, was overlaid with a scar, and often shed forth blood so that his tunic and drawers were sprinkled with sacred blood."

Even on the saint's death, the stigmata were still visible, as countless mourners who filed past the body witnessed. Many historians have dismissed St Francis's stigmata as an historical inaccuracy, but medical testimony on more recent cases of stigmata suggests that the story of St Francis could well have been true.

Another famous stigmatic is Padre Pio Forgione, a humble Capuchin friar. In 1915 he emerged from a long meditation with a stinging sensation in his hands. Three years later, just three days after celebrating the Feast of the Stigmata of St Francis, he was alone in the choir, when he suddenly let out a piercing cry. When his fellow friars rushed to his aid, they found him unconscious, and bleeding profusely from the traditional sites of all five of Jesus Christ's wounds – both hands, both feet and from his side, where Christ is believed to have received a wound from a spear. Padre Pio wrote of this first appearance of the stigmata, claiming that immediately prior to suffering the afflictions he had seen a vision:

"I saw before me a mysterious person . . . his hands and feet and side were dripping with blood. The vision disappeared and I became aware that my

Padre Pio, a famous stigmatic who shied away from publicity.

hands, feet and side were dripping blood. Imagine
the agony I experienced and continue to experience
almost every day."

Padre Pio was deeply embarrassed by his stigmata,
and begged for his symptoms to be kept secret, but
word soon spread and he found himself under almost
constant observation, not only from the Vatican, but
also from the worldwide media. Padre Pio suffered
from this affliction for fifty years. He would frequently
pass into an ecstatic state while celebrating mass, and
a cupful of blood would flow from his wounds every
day. He could only move with great pain and difficulty
right up to his death in 1968. There were those among
his fellow friars who claimed that they could pass their
fingers right through his wounds.

Although St Francis and Padre Pio are the two most
famous examples of stigmatics, it is a startling statistic
that over 80 per cent of all reported stigmatics have
been female. One such case is that of Heather Woods,
about whom both a television documentary was
filmed, and a book, *Spirit Within Her*, published.

Heather had, since the age of nine, been subjected to
physical, mental and sexual abuse in various care
homes. She had attempted suicide several times. Her
stigmata first appeared when she believed that she was
channelling spirits to produce drawings, and also
experiencing visions while in a trance-like state.
Heather fully believed that these visions were
bestowed upon her by God, and the drawings that
resulted were of Christ's crucifixion. On one occasion,
she envisioned herself on the cross inside the body of
Christ. Shortly after this amazing vision, Heather
received another drawing of Christ, this time being

baptized. When she came out of her trance-like state, she discovered that she had blisters on the palms and backs of both hands. Later that night, the blisters got bigger, and started to bleed. Heather spoke with her local priest, Father Eade, about the strange occurrence, and he immediately thought of stigmata, warning her to watch for signs of similar marks on her feet. When, a couple of days later, Heather's feet started to bleed, she became convinced that his theory was correct. The day after the marks appeared on her feet, Heather was visiting her sister. The two were lying in the garden when Heather suddenly felt that she had been bitten by an insect on her side. When she examined the "bite", she found a long red mark on her skin.

In time, the bleeding became quite profuse. Heather also noticed that the marks appeared to be weeping, something like water rather than blood running out of her sores for periods of up to three hours and, curiously, the wounds never scabbed over. Heather manifested one final stigma, many weeks after the initial wounds. During a service on St Luke's Day, a cross appeared on her forehead. It looked like a burn mark and was quite deep, and after about an hour it started to bleed. Heather visited her doctor about the mark, and he told her that it would take weeks to heal. Three days later, Heather awoke in the morning to discover that the mark on her forehead had disappeared completely, and that all the other marks had also gone. This was not the end, however, for the following year Heather again received a message through her channelling, which said that she would receive further stigmata eighteen days before Easter. In the early hours of the morning, exactly eighteen days before Easter, Heather awoke to find that the stigmata had indeed reappeared, and that her bed sheets were covered in blood.

There are several theories for the manifestation of stigmata. The first is simply that they are marks placed there by God either as a sign or, as many stigmatics have believed, to indicate a religious mission which they must undertake. Heather Woods firmly believed that she had been so marked as a sign for others that they should believe in her powers of healing. Another theory is that the stigmatics have somehow mutilated themselves in order to get attention, fame and money. This theory can be largely discounted because of the nature of the wounds, and also because, in most cases, the stigmatics themselves shy away from attention. The theory most in favour is that the appearance of the marks is a psychosomatic response to religious zeal. All recorded stigmatics have been Roman Catholics, and their stigmata have always reflected their beliefs in the manner of Christ's crucifixion. In the vast majority of cases, the appearance of the marks has occurred during, or immediately after, a moment of religious ecstasy, or while in a trance-like state. Another common feature among recipients of stigmata is a history of suffering of some sort, such as Heather Woods's abuse during childhood. It is argued that many stigmatics, faced with hardship or abuse, feel an affinity with Christ, the ultimate figure of trust, and that their mind afflicts their body with signs of His suffering. Again, this calls into question the power that the mind can have over the physical well-being of the body.

Meditation and yoga

Hindu and Buddhist traditions place an exceptionally high value on the practice of meditation, but it is also fairly common in Christianity, Islam, Judaism and other religions. The whole purpose of meditation is to calm, to detach oneself from the daily grind of life, and to seek an accord with something greater than the self. It is not thought of by practitioners as being a loss of consciousness, but rather as an expansion of consciousness, a means of accessing the subconscious. There have been many reports of psychic and paranormal powers resulting from meditation, and many who practise the art claim that it is a means of opening up one's psychic abilities.

Many people in the Western world view yoga simply as a means of relaxation. It is this, but is also so much more. The word "yoga" is Sanskrit for "union", and it is the union between the mind, soul and body of the individual with a cosmic entity that is the focus for most serious believers. The essence of what a practitioner, or *yogi*, aims to achieve through meditation is unity with the "Ground of All Being", which they believe is the cosmic force which created and upholds the universe.

There are many different forms of yoga, and one of the most commonly practised is the "kundalini", which deals with a belief in the existence of "chakras", thought to be centres of great psychic energy. Each chakra is associated with a part of the human body. In kundalini yoga, there are seven chakras, each responsible for invoking a different psychic power, as detailed in the table below. In kundalini yoga, the belief is that all human beings have hidden within them a powerful store of psychic energy. This is symbolized by a sleeping, coiled serpent, hidden within the *Muladhara* chakra. The techniques of kundalini yoga are attempts to arouse this sleeping snake, and then to get it to pass through all the other chakras. As the serpent passes through the various chakras, the yogi is bestowed with various *siddhis*, distinct psychic powers emanating from each individual chakra. Through complex breathing exercises, and the mental repetition of *mantras* (sacred chants), the power of the serpent is aroused. These exercises can take months or even years or decades to empower the serpent to complete its journey through all the chakras, and eventually finish in the *Sahasrara* chakra. A list of the powers bestowed by each chakra is detailed in the table opposite.

All manner of powers are believed to have been gained by yogis, including telepathy and clairvoyance, levitation and the ability to walk on water. Imperviousness to pain is one of the remarkable powers which is often associated with fakirs, who can lie for hours on beds of sharp nails without the slightest discomfort. This is yet another example of the mind's power over the physical body.

Immune to fire

All animals have an inbred fear of fire, and humankind is no different. Yet the mind power which some are able to draw upon, most often through some form of trance, can lead to astonishing physical accomplishments which seem to completely rewrite the body's ordinary set of rules.

Name of chakra	Area of the body associated with the chakra	Siddhi or power bestowed upon the individual
Muladhara	The perineum, between the genitals and anus	Control over the passions – lust, hate, envy, etc
Svadisthana	The pubic area	Complete control over the astral world
Manipura	The solar plexus	Powers associated with the rituals of white magic
Anahata	The cardiac plexus, the region of of the heart	Many and various, including clairvoyance and clairaudience
Vishuddha	The larynx and pharynx	Eternal wisdom
Ajna	Area from the middle of eyebrows to halfway down the nose	Liberation from karmic burdens accrued in past and present lives
Sahasrara	Area immediately above the crown the head	Yogi becomes a ruler of space and time

The immunity of certain rare people to extreme heat has been a source of wonder to observers of the phenomenon for centuries. The ability to resist fire has often been associated with religious fervour. In 1731 the Roman Catholic church began an investigation into an outbreak of "hysterical possession" associated with the death of a heretic named François de Paris. A group of de Paris's followers who were mourning his death were reported to have gone into convulsions, during which they contorted their limbs into seemingly impossible positions, and levitated. A magistrate, Carré de Montgeron, was appointed head of the board which was set up to examine these phenomena. He made detailed reports, which were corroborated by two priests and eight court officials. One of these reports told of a seemingly incombustible lady called Marie Souet. Montgeron reported how Marie had gone into a trance which rendered her body completely rigid. Wrapped only in a linen sheet, she was suspended over a raging fire for thirty-five minutes. Even though the flames physically lapped around her, neither she nor the sheet suffered any damage whatsoever. Montgeron was absolutely stunned by what he saw, and embarked on an investigation of the whole area of psychic ability. Unfortunately, this was not what the Roman Catholic church wanted, and he was condemned to the notorious prison, the Bastille, for his sympathetic attitude towards spiritism.

Another amazing account of someone who was apparently immune to fire was written by Lord Adare, the Earl of Dunraven, in 1868. He described the actions of Daniel Dunglas Home, a very famous medium of the nineteenth century, who was never discovered to have committed any fraud when demonstrating his remarkable powers. Lord Adare described how Home entered a trance, and became fascinated by the fireplace. Home repeatedly stirred the fire, until the embers burst into flame. He then knelt down and placed his face in the middle of the hot coals. Home then proceeded to pick up one of the hot coals and blow on it to make it glow red. What follows is Adare's account of a truly amazing spectacle – Home appeared to be able to extend his own immunity to fire to others:

> *"He came to me and said, 'Now, if you are not afraid, hold out your hand'; I did so, and having made two rapid passes over my hand, he placed the coal in it. I must have held it for half a minute, long enough to have burned my hand fearfully; the coal felt scarcely warm. Home then took it away, laughed, and seemed much pleased. As he was going back to the fireplace, he suddenly turned round and said, 'Why, just fancy, some of them think that only one side of the ember was hot.' He told me to make a hollow of both my hands; I did so, and he placed the coal in them, so that it was completely covered by our four hands, and we held it there for some time. Upon this occasion scarcely any heat at all could be perceived."*

There has been a long tradition of firewalking among fakirs, various Hindu sects and Buddhists. Every year, the people of Mbengga, a Fijian island, celebrate a truly astonishing ceremony. The night before the ceremony, the participants offer prayers and rites to the water god, Tui Namoliwai. Other islanders prepare a 25-foot-long (7.62 m) pit, which is 6 feet (1.83 m) deep. A pile of large stones is placed in the pit, and covered with a layer of logs, then a layer of brush, more stones, and a final layer of logs. This is then lit and left to burn all night. By the following morning, the heat from the pit is so intense that those who are responsible for attending to the fire must do so with long poles, and the stones are actively glowing with the heat.

The participants in the ceremony then file out one by one and, with no visible emotion on their faces, walk across the full length of the pit. It appears that the participants' mental preparation during the night before the ceremony is crucial to their ability to withstand the heat, otherwise the results can be horrific – in the 1940s, one firewalker was so badly injured that both legs had to be amputated. But such incidences are very rare among the Mbengga. So strong is the power of their mind that this has been the only recorded incident of harm during the annual ceremony's history. In 1950 Dr Wright of Philadelphia attended the ceremony and published his account of the fire walk. He wrote that the feet of two of the walkers, examined immediately before the walk, were sensitive to the approach of a burning cigarette, and showed no sign of having been coated with any form of protective substance. After the walk, the feet were examined again, and were covered in ash, but not burned or even blistered. The feet were, however, still sensitive to the approach of a burning cigarette. When asked for an explanation of this event Dr Wright could only repeat what the leader of the walk himself had said – "the water god sent hundreds of water babies to spread their bodies over the stones, and the men walked on the backs of the cool water babies".

The power of the mind over body can make people immune even to fire.

Science has tried to explain the phenomenon of fire-walking since Victorian times, but has yet to come up with anything concrete. Scientists refuse to believe that people are immune to fire, as this is surely a physical impossibility, and does not concur with modern scientific thinking. The only theory that holds any weight at all again refers back to the power of the mind over matter. Through meditation, or entering a trance, the firewalker generates power from his mind which controls the body, and enables the body to perform incredible feats.

Levitation

Ever since a chance apple happened to fall on Isaac Newton's head, the theory of gravity has been viewed as one of science's most infallible notions: what goes up must come down. We are all held to the Earth by the power of gravity, and will remain so without the help of some force to propel us from its surface. In spite of this, however, there are countless tales throughout history of those who have, in one way or another, overcome it and risen into the air. Often these levitations have been ascribed to religious fervour, as in the cases of St Joseph of Copertino and St Theresa of Avila.

St Joseph spent his youth trying to achieve religious ecstasy by such harsh means as self-flagellation, wearing horsehair shirts and voluntary starvation. His levitations were predominantly involuntary, apparently occurring every time he became emotionally excited. During a mass one Sunday, he flew into the air and on to the altar, burning himself quite badly on the candles as a result. He was banned from attending all public services for thirty-five years, but still his levitations continued. While walking with a monk in the gardens of the monastery, he suddenly rose into the air again, landing in an olive tree. Unfortunately for him, he couldn't fly back to ground level again, and had to wait in the tree until a ladder was brought to get him down.

St Theresa of Avila experienced violent levitations, so insistent that she begged her fellow sisters to hold her down when she felt herself rising from the floor. St Theresa wrote of her experiences, and described the feelings she had when suffering her gravity-defying attacks:

> "It seemed to me, when I tried to make some resistance, as if a great force beneath my feet lifted me up. I confess that it threw me into great fear, very great indeed at first; for in seeing one's body thus lifted up from the earth, though the spirit draws it upwards after itself (and that with great sweetness, if unresisted), the senses are not lost; at least I was so much myself as able to see that I was being lifted up."

Levitation is commonly associated with Indian fakirs. The *Illustrated London News* ran an article on a famous Indian yogi, Subbayah Pullavar, in 1936. Around 150 impartial witnesses were gathered together to watch the fakir perform a levitation, and one of them, P. Y. Plunkett, has left us a full account of the event. A tent had been set up, and water was poured around it. No one was allowed to enter the circle of water wearing leather-soled shoes, and the fakir entered the tent alone. A few minutes later some helpers removed the tent, and there, inside the circle of water, was the fakir, floating in mid-air. Plunkett and another witness stepped forward to examine Pullavar, who was suspended about a metre from the ground. They examined the space around him, and found no strings or any other apparatus which could possibly have supported his weight. Pullavar remained in this position for about four minutes, and then the tent was placed around him, and he began a slow, swaying descent, which Plunkett witnessed through the thin tent walls.

For the most famous account of levitation, we must return once again to the Victorian spiritualist, Daniel Dunglas Home. The incident in question is still the subject of debate in the scientific community, particularly since it was documented by three respectable witnesses: Lord Adare, Captain Wynne and the Master of Lindsay. The latter of these three described an event during which Home levitated out of the window of one room, and back in through the window of another:

> *"During the sitting Mr Home went into a trance and in that state was carried out of the window in the room next to where we were, and was brought in at our window. The distance between the windows was about 7 feet 6 inches (2.29 m), and there was not the slightest foothold between them, nor was there more than a 12-inch (0.3 m) projection to each window, which served as a ledge to put flowers on. We heard the window in the next room lift up, and almost immediately after we saw Home floating in the air outside the window. The moon was shining full into the room; my back was to the*

light, and I saw the shadow on the wall of the windowsill, and Home's feet about 6 inches (0.15 m) above it. He remained in this position for a few seconds, then raised the window and glided into the room feet foremost and sat down."

Home made a career out of his amazing abilities, performing over 1500 recorded séances, and was never exposed as a fraud. His most famous feat remains the one detailed above, and for this we have but three witnesses. The event has been viewed as extremely special to many, and very suspicious to others. Author, sceptic and debunker of the paranormal, Archie Jarman sought to prove Home's finest hour as a hoax in an article for *Alpha* magazine in October 1980, 112 years after the event.

Jarman found the house where the alleged levitation occurred, and examined it thoroughly. He noticed an architectural feature which none of the three witnesses had mentioned in their accounts – a ledge about 5 inches (0.13 m) wide which ran just below two balconies. Jarman tried to cross between the two balconies using the ledge, but soon gave up. It was impossible to cross using only that ledge. Jarman also put forward the possibility that Home had used some form of tightrope to make the passage between the balconies, but again, could not do it for himself. The conclusion of Jarman's article was that there could be no conclusion. The event was witnessed by three very respectable gentlemen, but this is hardly scientific proof. However, hundreds of people did in fact witness Home levitate in drawing rooms throughout Europe and America in his time. There was no doubt in their minds that the levitations were genuine phenomena, and that Hume was possessed of incredible powers which defied human understanding.

It is very hard to believe that everyone who claims an ability to defy gravity is performing an elaborate hoax. The fact that science struggles to explain something does not deny its existence. Whether the ability to levitate is a psychic power, an ability given by the spirits or a remarkable feat of the mind is a question to which as yet there is no answer.

Hypnotism/mesmerism

Hypnosis is generally defined as a form of trance, an altered state of consciousness, during which an individual or even a group will come under the influence of another. To what extent a hypnotist can be said to "control" the mind of another has been the subject of debate for over 200 years. Hypnosis appears to turn off some part of our minds that ordinarily controls our behaviour, instructing us to do something without thought on our own part. This control is handed over to the hypnotist.

Although hypnotism has been practised in tribal societies throughout history, it only really came to prominence in Western societies through the work of Franz Mesmer (hence, "mesmerism") 200 years ago. Mesmer made two discoveries of great significance. First, he found that if he told a patient who was in a trance that he would feel no pain, he would indeed feel no pain. Mesmer showed that surgical operations could be performed without any discomfort to the patient, and this was before the discovery of anaesthetics. Mesmer was shunned by the medical profession at the time. Leading physicians were invited to watch him perform the amputation of a leg, and on seeing that the patient, who was awake throughout the operation, felt no pain, they insisted that he was merely pretending not to feel any pain. Quite an actor by any accounts. Mesmer's other discovery was that some of his hypnotized subjects acquired talents while under his spell which they did not possess in ordinary life. Some became adept at drawing, and a few appeared to gain clairvoyant capabilities, describing events that they could not possibly have witnessed.

Hypnotism seems to access parts of the mind that are ordinarily dormant. Research has shown that, under hypnotic trance, individuals can become immune to the effects of fire, in much the same way as the firewalkers above. Conversely, if a hypnotized subject is told that he is going to be touched with a red-hot skewer, he will cry out in pain if touched by a cold implement and, more startlingly, will blister where the cold tool touched his skin. Hypnotic regression is a fairly recent discovery. People under a hypnotic trance have been able to access memories deeply hidden in the subconscious in tremendous detail. This has been used extensively by police when questioning crime victims. One of the most exciting and fascinating of psychic phenomena, however, is hypnotic regression into alleged past lives.

During the 1950s an American hypnotist, Morey Bernstein, performed an experiment on a certain Virginia Tighe. Mrs Tighe was regressed under hypnosis and told a truly fascinating story, seemingly of a past life. Under suggestion, Mrs Tighe began to speak with an Irish accent and claimed that she was Bridie Murphy, the daughter of Duncan and Kathleen

Murphy, living in Cork almost 200 years ago. Her tale included incredible detail. She claimed that in 1818 she married a Roman Catholic and that they set up home together in Belfast. The couple shopped at stores which "Bridie" named, identifying the correct coins for the period, and worshipped together at St Theresa's church. She was well versed in Irish mythology, knew Irish songs and described in detail the correct procedure for kissing the Blarney stone. All of this is quite remarkable when one considers that Virginia Tighe had never visited Ireland in her (present) life.

A journalist called William Barker was commissioned by *Empire* magazine to investigate Mrs Tighe's story. He spent three weeks in Ireland checking the facts that Mrs Tighe had given under hypnosis. In a 19,000-word report, his findings could not prove either way for certain that Bridie's case was genuine. He could not find any birth or marriage records relating to a Bridie Murphy, because no records were kept in Cork until 1864. He could not uncover the existence of St Theresa's church, but did find two shops which were described in detail by Bridie. The case has never been proven to be either genuine or fake.

A famous hypnotherapist called Arnall Bloxham regressed one subject back to six previous lives, in a famous BBC broadcast in the 1970s. Jane Evans was the subject in question, and what is particularly fascinating about her case is the detail that she gave while under hypnosis of her "past lives", most of which, when checked, proved to be accurate.

Jane Evans's first regression took her back to AD 286. Here, she claimed that she was Livonia, wife of Titus, the tutor to the Roman emperor Constantine. She described how she and her husband lived at Eboracum (the Roman name for York), and how they were both converted to Christianity. An expert on Roman Britain was called in to corroborate this story, and he claimed that "Livonia" knew some "quite remarkable historical facts".

Jane Evans's second "life" was much less glittering. No longer associated with the upper echelons of Roman society, she was now a Jewess called Rebecca. In 1190, she claimed that she was murdered in the crypt of St Mary's church, York, together with many other Jews. At the time that she was regressed, this past life was discredited because there was no known crypt at St Mary's church. A few years later, however, archaeologists uncovered the crypt, and Jane's story suddenly became very credible indeed.

Sceptics have readily discounted her third life as the servant of a French merchant prince called Jacques Coeur, because much has been written about him, and she could easily have acquired this knowledge from her local library. In this instance, her regression uncovered nothing out of the ordinary, save for a detailed knowledge of medieval French history.

Life number four saw Jane returning to the highest echelons of society once again. This time, she was Anna, the lady-in-waiting to Catherine of Aragon, first wife of Henry VIII. Again her historical facts were accurate, but she revealed nothing that could not be discovered by a visit to the local library. The same was also true of her fifth regression as Anne Tasker, a seamstress in London at the end of the seventeenth century.

Her final regression saw her as Sister Grace, a nineteenth-century nun in Iowa. Again, Jane showed a remarkable knowledge of events contemporary to the time, but little else. Many sceptics have looked at the case of Jane Evans and have pointed to one obvious omission. Although Mrs Evans, while under hypnosis, fully believed that she was a previous incarnation, she did not speak the language of that past life. Whether an ancient Roman, a medieval French lady or an American nun, she always spoke in English. Arnall Bloxham did say, however, that the vast majority of subjects under hypnosis do not take on the language of their previous incarnations. Jane Evans did pronounce the names of cities and people according to the language of her past life.

The debate over past lives is a fierce one indeed, as it can be thought of essentially as an argument over the immortality of the soul. This is discussed in depth in Chapter 5. Regression to past lives is, as we have seen, only a part of the whole sphere of hypnosis. Regardless of the arguments over this aspect of it, the indisputable fact is that some people have the power to create in their subjects a state of mind during which some individuals show incredible capabilities.

Spontaneous human combustion

Although, technically speaking, spontaneous human combustion is not a psychic power, one case merits investigation. All recorded cases of this horrifying fate have several things in common. Firstly, victims of spontaneous human combustion have been reduced to a heap of carbonized ashes within minutes – suggesting incomprehensibly intense heat. The human body is very hard to set alight under normal circumstances. All experts agree that in order to reduce the human body to ashes, a fierce heat needs to be applied to it for hours, and even crematoria have to grind bones after incineration. It takes a heat of about 5432°F (3000°C) to melt bones. Yet with almost all cases of human combustion, practically the entire body (often save a limb or two) has been totally reduced to ash. The second curiosity that most cases have in common is the unusual confinement of the heat. With such intense temperatures, one would expect entire buildings to succumb to the effects of the fire, but in most instances of spontaneous human combustion, the fire has not spread at all. In a few cases, the victim's clothes have even remained intact, or only slightly charred. There is, therefore, more to spontaneous human combustion than initially meets the eye, as if that weren't enough. Some psychic or psychological phenomenon accompanies the burning, rendering most victims powerless to escape, and those few who have survived unable to tell what happened to them.

From a psychic point of view, the most amazing case of spontaneous combustion occurred one hundred years ago. It has been hailed as a case of truly tragic coincidence by some, and proof of a cosmic link, telepathy, or empathy by others. The case concerned two sisters, aged respectively four and five. Their parents were separated, and one sister lived with their mother, the other with their father. In 1899, the two sisters, who lived a mile apart, both burst into flames in their houses at exactly the same time. No matches or anything that could have started the fires were ever found. Was this just a tragic coincidence, or were the two girls linked in some tragic way that we will never be able to understand?

Mind Over Matter

●●

Prophecy

Tales of prophetic visions, foreseers of the future, have existed for as long as humankind. There are tales of such phenomena occurring in all cultures' folklore, in the writings of the ancient Egyptians, Greeks and Romans, and in the Bible. Oracles were an integral part of life in the ancient world, both respected and revered by all levels of society.

The ancient Greeks firmly believed that these oracles could see into the future. One tale which has passed down through the years is that of King Croesus of Lydia. Croesus needed the help of an oracle to divine how to defeat his powerful enemies, the Persians, but he had a dilemma – which oracle to choose? At the time, there were six oracles in Greece and one in Egypt, all of which were reported to be extremely accurate. Croesus decided to test the mettle of these oracles, and sent out seven messengers, one to each of the great prophets. He told each messenger to pose the same question, exactly one hundred days after they were sent. The question they were to ask was, "What is King Croesus doing right now?" Each messenger was then to return to Croesus and tell him what the oracle had said.

As a result of this test, Croesus decided to place all his trust in the oracle at Delphi. The oracle had passed on the following message to Croesus's messenger:

> *"I can count the sands, and I can measure the ocean;*
> *I have ears for the silent and know what the dumb man meaneth;*
> *Lo! On my sense there striketh the smell of a shell-covered tortoise,*
> *Boiling now on a fire, with the flesh of a lamb in a cauldron –*
> *Brass is the vessel below, and brass the cover above it."*

Croesus really knew how to test an oracle's ability. Exactly one hundred days after sending out his messengers, he decided to do something which no one could possibly guess, something truly out of the ordinary. He had taken a tortoise and a lamb, cut them into pieces and boiled them in a brass cauldron with a brass lid.

Another well-known prophet was a young farm labourer who lived in fifteenth-century England, called Robert Nixon. He was thought of by his fellow Cheshire villagers as being mentally retarded, and was prone to babbling incomprehensibly. One day, however, the words he spoke brought him immediate fame. While ploughing the fields, he suddenly stopped what he was doing and said, "Now Dick! Now Harry! Oh, ill done Dick! Oh well done Harry! Harry has gained the day!" At the time, his fellow workers dismissed these words as another of Crazy Bob's babblings, but the next day, news arrived which put his words into perspective. At the very same time that Robert had downed tools to utter these rants, King Richard III had been slain at the Battle of Bosworth Field. The victor, Henry Tudor, was to become king of England – Harry had indeed gained the day.

News of Robert Nixon's amazing prophecy soon reached the newly crowned king, who ordered him to London immediately. Before the king's messenger had even left London, however, Robert became very distressed and claimed to his friends that King Henry had sent for him, and that he would starve to death. Despite his fears, he accompanied the envoy to London, where King Henry had prepared a test for his strange powers. When Robert was ushered in to the king's chambers, the king made a show of appearing very upset. He claimed that he had lost a very valuable diamond and needed Robert's help to find it. Robert simply replied that those who can hide, can find. Obviously, the king had hidden the diamond in the first place, not lost it, and he was so impressed by Robert's answer that he ordered that everything Robert said should be written down from that point on. Robert predicted the English civil wars and their outcome, the deaths of future kings of England, and that England would go to war with France, all of which came to be. He also predicted that Nantwich, a town in Cheshire, would be destroyed by a flood although, nearly 500 years later, this is yet to happen.

Robert became a favourite of the king but he was constantly troubled by his earlier prophecy – that he would starve to death in the royal palace. The king therefore ordered his kitchen staff to provide Robert with whatever food he wanted, whenever he wanted it. This made Robert extremely unpopular with the kitchen staff, and the other courtiers who were jealous of his extra privileges. Soon afterwards, the king left London, leaving one of his officers in charge of caring for Robert, and in particular, to ensure that no harm came to him because of envious courtiers and staff. To protect him, the officer locked him safely in one of the king's cupboards. Unfortunately, the officer was then called away to join the king, and forgot to mention where Robert was hidden. When he and the king returned, some weeks later, they found Robert still in the cupboard, starved to death.

The most famous of all prophets is a Frenchman named Michel de Nostredame, known now simply as "Nostradamus". Nostradamus was educated as a physician, and was noted for his work during the plagues of the sixteenth century, but his real fame was achieved through his writing. He first published a book entitled *The Prognostications*, which was basically an almanac of weather predictions for the following year, but his ten collections of prophecies, *The Centuries*, are what he is most famous for. Nostradamus wrote his prophecies in verse – almost 1000 four-line verses, and a collection of six-line verses. The verses are not in chronological order, and the vast majority of them use heavy symbolism and seem very obscure, which is why so much controversy surrounds them – are they really predictions of the future, or can anything be read into them if you try hard enough? Nostradamus himself gave an explanation for this, claiming that the use of symbolism and the lack of chronology was deliberately done to avoid persecution by the Spanish Inquisition, whom he feared would accuse him of heresy, or even witchcraft. Another reason for the obscure symbolism is that Nostradamus's visions seem to span thousands of years – it would have been difficult to describe twentieth-century technology using sixteenth-century French.

There has been much conjecture over the nature of many of Nostradamus's prophecies, as most of them are so vague. Some, however, are much clearer, and definitely seem to point clearly to events that had not yet occurred when *The Centuries* was written, but which did come true later. The very first prophecy that brought fame for Nostradamus is the following:

> *"The young lion will overcome the older one, in a field of combat in single fight: He will pierce his eyes in their golden cage; two wounds in one, then he dies a cruel death."*

Henri II of France took part in a jousting contest in 1559, against Montgomery, the captain of the Scottish Guard. During this bout, Montgomery's lance pierced the king's gilt helmet and entered his head, just above the eye. He also suffered a second wound to the throat, and his death was indeed cruel – he lay in agony for ten days before he finally passed away. Henri also used to display the lion as his emblem.

This prediction brought Nostradamus instant fame, but his prediction of the death of Henri III was even closer to the truth:

> *"That which neither weapon nor flame could accomplish will be achieved by a sweet sleeping tongue in council. Sleeping, in a dream, the king will see the enemy not in war or of military blood."*

Henri III was indeed killed in council, and not in war.

A monk, Jacques Clément, came to the king, pretending that he had a secret letter for him. As the monk leant towards Henri, pretending to whisper in his ear, he stabbed him in the stomach. Three days before his death, the king had told his courtiers that he had dreamed of this monk treading his royal effects underfoot, and that he thought that this was an augury of his death.

The problem with interpreting Nostradamus's prophecies is that he very rarely gave any clue as to when the events he foresaw would take place. All his visions are subject to conjecture and interpretation, and a fuller discussion is offered in Chapter 12 – on Nostradamus's predictions concerning the Great Fire of London, Hitler, the Kennedys and, worryingly, Armageddon.

Clairvoyance

The term "prophet" seems, in the modern world, outdated, and most psychics would rather call their ability to see into the future "clairvoyance", though, personally, I would think that the terms are to an extent interchangeable. From the earliest prophets right through to today's clairvoyants, the most common visions experienced seem to be connected with disasters. With such premonitions, could tragedies be averted, or does the clairvoyant's vision enable them to see, but not act?

In 1979, a hotel executive in Spain called Jaime Castell dreamed that he would never see his unborn child, which was expected in three months' time. Jaime became convinced that he was going to die, and took out a £50,000 insurance policy, payable only on his death, with no remuneration if he lived. Weeks later, he was driving home from work at a safe, constant 50 mph (80 kph), when another car travelling in the opposite direction at over 100 mph (160 kph) skidded out of control, hit a safety barrier and landed on top of Jaime's car, killing him instantly. The insurance company told Mr Castell's widow that a death occurring so soon after a policy had been taken out would have to be investigated thoroughly. The investigation showed that there were no suspicious circumstances connected with the accident – a fraction of a second either way and Jaime would have escaped. Jaime had foreseen his death, and there was nothing he could have done to prevent the tragedy happening.

On 20 October 1966, a nine-year-old Welsh girl, Eryl Mai Jones, told her mother that she had had a dream that when she had gone to school it was not there, that something black had come down all over it. The following day a terrible tragedy occurred in the Welsh mining village of Aberfan, where Eryl lived. Half a million tons of coal waste from a nearby slag heap fell down on to the village, destroying the school, and taking the lives of 139 people, mostly children, and including Eryl. An entire generation was wiped out in the awful calamity. After the tragedy, many people claimed to have foreseen it, and again, nothing could possibly have been done to avert the disaster.

The great majority of premonitions are only made public after the event to which they refer has happened – "I saw that coming, honest." There is obviously a good deal of scope for hoaxes, as anyone could say that they had had a vision about an event the night before, once the event has already happened. The most amazing and best-known prophecy ever made is probably the story of the *Titanic*, the "safest ocean liner ever built", which sank on her maiden voyage in 1912.

Morgan Robertson was born in 1861 in New York, and grew up to become a writer. At the age of thirty-six, he told friends that he was convinced that he was not actually doing the writing himself, but that he was being channelled by spirit guides, who were doing the writing for him. In 1898, he published his first novel, *The Wreck of the Titan, or Futility*. In the story, a 70,000-tonne ship, the safest ocean liner in the world, hit an iceberg in the Atlantic on her maiden voyage and sank. Most of the ship's 2500 passengers were killed because the liner had only twenty-four lifeboats, fewer than half the number required to save the lives of all the passengers and crew. We all know the tragedy of the *Titanic*, but Robertson's augury in his novel is astounding. Opposite is a table which shows the similarities between the *Titan* (the name of the ship in the novel) and the real *Titanic*.

The comparison between the work of fiction and the grim reality is truly astounding. Sceptics, who believe that the novel's connection to the *Titanic* is merely a coincidence, point out the differences between the two. For example the *Titan* struck the iceberg in thick fog, but the *Titanic* struck the iceberg on a clear night; where the *Titan* became grounded on the iceberg, the *Titanic* struck it and sailed on. They also point out that many of the coincidences might have been predictable – April is the most dangerous month for icebergs in the North Atlantic because the warmer temperatures of spring cause them to break free from glaciers.

But some of the similarities are much more difficult

TITAN	TITANIC
The ship was British, but owned by a company whose main shareholder was a wealthy American	The ship was British and owned by White Star Line, whose main shareholder was J.P. Morgan, a wealthy American
Regarded as "unsinkable"	Claimed by the shipbuilders to be "practically unsinkable"
Top speed 25 knots	Top speed around 23–25 knots
800 feet (244 m) long	882 feet (268 m) long
2000 passengers aboard	2227 (approx) passengers aboard
24 lifeboats on the ship	20 lifeboats on the ship
40,000 horsepower	50,000 horsepower
Struck iceberg, leading to sinking	Struck iceberg, leading to sinking
Huge loss of life	Estimated 1522 died
Happened on an April night	Happened on an April night
Sea waters were calm	Sea waters were calm
Was travelling at a very high speed	Was trying to better the time of her sister ship
Happened in the North Atlantic off Newfoundland Banks	Happened in the North Atlantic off Newfoundland Banks
Three propellers	Three propellers
Ship had nineteen watertight compartments	Ship had fifteen watertight compartments

to explain rationally. The fact that both the fictional and the real ships were on their maiden voyages and the fact that the seas were calm – how can these be easily explained? The fact is that the sceptics have only one real line of defence – that if the novel was not channelled by spirit guides as an augury of a future tragedy, then Robertson had in fact written a story about a shipping tragedy which mirrored a real-life disaster of fourteen years later, by pure coincidence alone. Frankly, I find the theory of the spirit guides much easier to accept, especially in the light of one of Robertson's later novels. In 1909, he wrote about a war between the USA and Japan that started because of a surprise attack on the American Navy, while the fleet was in the harbour. It does not take an enormous leap of imagination to link this with the events at Pearl Harbor in 1941, when the American fleet was the victim of a surprise attack by the Japanese and which launched the USA into World War II.

A very famous clairvoyant who worked under the professional name of "Cheiro" also made a prediction related to the *Titanic*. He warned English journalist William Stead that he should avoid travelling by water in mid April 1912. Stead was among those who drowned on 14 April 1912 as a result of the sinking of the *Titanic*.

Prior to this event, Cheiro was summoned to Russia by the "Mad Monk" Rasputin, in 1905. Cheiro predicted the following:

> *"I foresee for you a violent end within the palace. You will be menaced by poison, by knife and by bullet. Finally, I see the icy waters of the Neva closing above you."*

Rasputin, a renowned hypnotist and healer, was the most feared and detested person in Russia at the time, because of his hold over the Russian royal family, who believed that he had miraculously saved the life of their son. Nine years after Cheiro's prediction, Rasputin was stabbed in the stomach by a peasant woman, although he survived the attack. In a letter to the Russian Czar Nicholas II, he made a prophecy himself:

> "If I am killed by common assassins, and especially by my brothers the Russian peasants, you . . . have nothing to fear. But if I am murdered by Boyars [Russian nobles], and if they shed my blood, their hands will remain soiled with my blood . . . Brothers will kill brothers and they will kill each other and . . . there will be no nobles in the country."

Two years later, in December 1916, Rasputin was invited to Prince Felix Yusupov's palace. Several noblemen had, in fact, plotted his murder, and arranged for him to be the first to arrive. When he did arrive, wine and cake had been laid out for him, and he helped himself to generous amounts of both, completely unaware that they were laced with cyanide. Unfortunately for the conspirators, Rasputin was totally unaffected by the usually fast-acting, fatal poison. When Yusupov arrived and found Rasputin alive and well, he shot him in the back, and Rasputin was pronounced dead. The conspirators picked up the "corpse", with the intention of disposing of the body in the Neva river, but the "Mad Monk" sprang to life and made to attack Yusupov. He was shot twice more, kicked and battered. The plotters then took his body to the Neva, cut a hole in the ice and threw Rasputin into the water. Incredibly, Rasputin was still breathing when he was thrown in. With Rasputin's death, two prophecies were fulfilled. His own vision of the future, as detailed above, was soon realized with the bloody Russian Revolution the following year. The accuracy of Cheiro's foretelling of the manner of his death is plain to see.

In 1925, Cheiro made another incredible prediction, this time in connection with the then Prince of Wales, Edward. Cheiro said, "It is within the range of possibility that he will fall victim of a devastating love affair. If he does, I predict the prince will give up everything, even the chance of being crowned, rather than lose the object of his affection." Nine years later, King George V died and the Prince of Wales was expected to be crowned Edward VIII. Less than a year later, he abdicated from the throne in favour of his lover and future wife, the twice-divorced Mrs Wallis Simpson, in one of the biggest scandals ever to beset the British monarchy.

Even the most celebrated of clairvoyants would never say that they are 100 per cent correct with their predictions. Most would argue that they have roughly a 70 per cent success rate, and sceptics generally say that the reason that this is so high is because the vast majority of predictions are incredibly vague. Naturally, sceptics would say that it is totally impossible for anyone to see into the future, and that until such time as precognition can be proven under laboratory conditions, they will never believe in it. But this is a very myopic point of view. There are some astounding accounts on record that cannot possibly be explained by science (yet), but surely the lack of scientific understanding does not deny their existence?

Sam Clemens, better known as Mark Twain, worked as an apprentice pilot on a steamboat on the Mississippi river, before he became famous as the creator of *Huckleberry Finn* and *Tom Sawyer*. Sam's younger brother, Henry, worked on the same boat, the Pennsylvania, as a clerk. While visiting his sister in St Louis, Sam had a premonition, a very vivid dream. He saw a metal coffin resting on two chairs, and lying in the coffin was his brother, Henry. Resting on Henry's chest was a bouquet of white flowers with one crimson flower at the centre.

A few days later Sam returned to work, but fell out with the chief pilot of the *Pennsylvania*. He was duly transferred to another steamboat, the *Lacey*. Henry remained on board the *Pennsylvania*, which was travelling up the Mississippi two days ahead of the *Lacey*. When Sam reached his destination, he was informed that the *Pennsylvania* had blown up, causing the deaths of 150 people, but his brother was still alive, though in a critical condition. Sam spent the next six days with Henry, until his brother passed away. Sam was exhausted, and fell asleep at Henry's deathbed. When he awoke, his brother's body had been removed, and he went to look for it, finding it in another room. Just as in his dream, Sam saw his brother's body, resting in a metal coffin that had been placed on two chairs, but there was no bouquet of flowers. As Sam sat by his brother's side, an elderly lady entered the room, carrying a bouquet of white flowers with a single red rose at the centre. She placed them on Henry's chest, and left.

Even the most hardened of sceptics must surely see that this is more than just a coincidence, or an example of a charlatan seeking fame by fraudulent means?

What could Mark Twain possibly have hoped to gain by creating a fiction out of the untimely death of his brother? Nothing.

The politics of ESP

Three of the world's most famous politicians all believed in psychic powers and, more impressively, utilized them themselves. Abraham Lincoln is reported to have taken advice from mediums, and many believe that American slaves owe their freedom to spirit messages which were passed on to the former president by Nettie Colburn Maynard. While in a trance-like state, Nettie allegedly lectured the president for an hour on the importance of freeing the slaves. Lincoln also experienced the paranormal on a far more personal level. One day he awoke after experiencing a very vivid dream. In the dream, he had heard the sound of crying, and had followed it through the White House until he reached a room where he found a coffin draped with the stars and stripes. In his dream, the president asked a soldier who was standing guard over the coffin who had died, and the soldier replied, "It's the president, he has been assassinated." Days later, on Good Friday, 14 April 1865, Lincoln famously visited Ford's Theatre in Washington where he was assassinated by John Wilkes Booth.

The two great wartime leaders, Winston Churchill and Franklin Roosevelt also believed in, and experienced, psychic phenomena. Churchill was holding a dinner party at 10 Downing Street during World War II when he suddenly had a premonition. He rose out of his chair and went through to the kitchen, instructing the butler to put the dinner on a hot plate in the dining room, and then make his way with the rest of the kitchen staff to the bomb shelter. Three minutes later, a bomb fell at the back of the house, utterly destroying the kitchen.

In 1941, Churchill was visiting an anti-aircraft battery. When the visit was over, he returned to his car in order to leave, and the passenger door was opened for him by the driver, as always. He ignored the open door, went round to the other side of the car, and got in there. Minutes later, a bomb exploded close by, forcing the car on to two wheels. Churchill said that "it must have been my beef on that side that pulled it down". When his wife asked him about the incident, Churchill told her, "Something said 'Stop!' before I reached the car door held open for me. It then appeared to me that I was told I was meant to open the door on the other side and get in and sit there – and that's what I did." Was this just a hunch, a coincidence, or a premonition? We will never know, but Churchill had learned throughout his life to obey his intuitive powers, and to great effect.

Churchill's wartime ally, Franklin Roosevelt, is known to have consulted a psychic, Jeane Dixon, who was known as the "Washington seer". Dixon's greatest fame, however, was achieved for her prediction about the death of John F. Kennedy. In 1952 she had a vision of the White House with a young, blue-eyed man standing in the door and, at the same time, she heard a warning that a Democrat who would be inaugurated as president in 1960 would be assassinated while in office. In 1960, John F. Kennedy became the youngest-ever president of the United States. Early in 1963, Dixon began to have new premonitions about the president's safety and made several attempts to warn him of the danger she had foreseen. On the morning of 22 November that year, she told friends, "This is the day it will happen." That afternoon, Kennedy was assassinated.

Five years later, Jeane Dixon was addressing a meeting in the Ambassador Hotel in Los Angeles. A journalist in the audience asked her if Robert Kennedy would ever become president of the United States. Her answer was to prove most prophetic:

"No, he will never become president of the United States because of a tragedy right here in this hotel."

One week later, Robert Kennedy won the California primary election. He had just finished addressing a victory rally in the Ambassador Hotel when he was shot. He died the following day.

Telepathy

Telepathy is a form of psychic communication – that is, communication between two minds without the use of speech, sign language, body language or written media. The range of telepathic communication is quite wide. Some people report hearing actual words in their heads, while others claim to receive emotions rather than actual sentences. One of the biggest areas of research into telepathy lies in the testing of twins, who are widely believed to have a much greater extra-sensory connection with each other than most people. Even if identical twins are separated from each other at birth and brought up in totally different environments, they will often develop the same tastes and attitudes.

Professor Bouchard of the University of Minneapolis conducted extensive research into this phenomenon. One set of identical twins whom he investigated was Bridget Harrison and Dorothy Lowe. These identical sisters were born in England in 1945, and separated a few weeks later. They were not reunited until 1979, when they came to the attention of Professor Bouchard. When they met each other and Professor Bouchard (for he brought them together), they were both wearing seven rings and two bracelets. Not only that, further research showed other startling "coincidences". Both women loved reading historical romance novels. Dorothy's favourite author turned out to be Catherine Cookson, and Bridget's was Caroline Marchant. Caroline Marchant is one of Catherine Cookson's pseudonyms. Dorothy's son was called "Richard Andrew", and Bridget's was called "Andrew Richard". They had also both kept a diary in the year 1960. Neither of them had kept a diary before 1960, nor had they kept a diary in any year after 1960. Their diaries were the same make and colour and, most startlingly, they had both filled in exactly the same days in their respective diaries. If 21 January was blank in Bridget's diary, it was blank in Dorothy's also. Discussion of coincidence stretches the bounds of credibility in this case: there are far too many similarities over too many years for coincidence to be used as a valid interpretation. Only two possible explanations remain: did they both make the same choices in their lives because of genetic make-up, or was telepathy involved?

Another case which defies scientific explanation, even genetics, is that of identical twins, Nancy and

Ruth Schneider. During their examinations for college, the twins were sitting apart from each other in the exam room. Both chose the same question for an essay. Nothing overly remarkable about that, but both wrote the same essay – *exactly* the same essay, word for word.

It is not only twins who are believed to experience telepathic communications. In 1955, a young girl called Joicey Hurth of Cedarburg, Wisconsin, returned home from a friend's birthday party. Her mother told her that her father and two brothers had just left to watch a film, and the girl dashed off to the cinema to watch it with them. A few minutes after she had left, her mother called the cinema. She was convinced that her daughter had been in an accident, but she didn't know how she knew. The attendant at the cinema was stunned by the telephone call, saying to Mrs Hurth, "How did you know? It – the accident – just happened." Joicey had in fact run into the path of a car just outside the cinema, and was not badly hurt. When she told of her experience, she said that she called out in her mind, "Mama, mama, mama!" Parapsychologists who studied the case said that since Mrs Hurth neither saw nor heard anything that could have made her aware of her daughter's plight, the only way that she could have known that she had to make the call to the cinema was through telepathy.

Science may shun the existence of telepathy, but it has been secretly experimented with for military and espionage purposes, particularly by America and the Soviet Union during the Cold War. In the late 1950s, telepathy hit the news in a big way. The French press published reports that successful telepathy tests had been carried out between an American agent on land,

and a subject on board the submarine USS *Nautilus*. The United States vigorously denied the story, but their Russian counterparts took it very seriously indeed.

The Soviets made public the work of their top psychical investigators, work which had been top secret for over thirty years. The most acclaimed of these parapsychologists was Dr Leonid Vasiliev, who claimed that he had been ordered on the very highest authority to research psychic phenomena. This suggests that Stalin may have been keen to study the possibilities of telepathy for military purposes. Dr Vasiliev used hypnotized subjects to investigate telepathy. He revealed that he and other researchers had been able to make hypnotized people carry out actions by telepathic order. He was able to demonstrate this mental communication even under laboratory conditions. These experiments were taken further by the Russians, and have astounded scientists and sceptics alike. Biophysicist Yuri Kamensky, and Moscow journalist Karl Nikolaiev, performed a series of tests to demonstrate their psychic powers. In one of these tests, Nikolaiev correctly described six objects that had been given to Kamensky. Nikolaiev was wired to an electroencephalograph, which monitored his brain waves. As soon as Kamensky began to transmit images, Nikolaiev's brain waves altered. The two people were 2000 miles (3218 km) apart at the time.

Psychokinesis or poltergeists?

Stories of poltergeists, mischievous spirits who physically move objects, have been around for centuries. Unlike tales of other hauntings, poltergeists have a tendency to pester a person rather than a place. If the occupants of a haunted house leave, the ghost will stay, but in poltergeist cases the spirit tends to follow them wherever they go. Although cases have shown that poltergeists can be destructive, evidence has shown that they have rarely caused any injury to people. They tend to act more like children seeking attention, just trying to get someone to notice them. These points, coupled with the fact that the vast majority of poltergeist cases centre around a young teenage girl, have led to a split in parapsychologists' thinking. A great majority of parapsychologists now believe that such cases are attributable to psychic powers in the mind of the affected subject rather than a visitation from the spirit world. In other words, the subject has the power of psychokinesis. Other investigators still believe in ghostly intervention, and exorcisms to expel the poltergeist still take place.

We shall first look at evidence for the latter school of thought. In 1967, Matthew Manning became involved in a series of events that were to change his life. Objects about the Manning household began to move mysteriously. At first they were very minor occurrences – coffee tables found a few metres out of position, cups that should have been on shelves were discovered on the floor. Matthew's parents put this down to pranks on Matthew's part, but over a period of time the happenings grew stranger. Tapping, creaking and knockings on the walls were heard at night and during the day, often occurring in more than one part of the house at a time, something which Matthew would obviously not have been able to do, no matter how mischievous. Matthew's parents eventually sought the help of a psychical researcher, Dr Owen, who told them that the events they had experienced were typical of a poltergeist encounter. He also told them that poltergeists are difficult to remove from a house, unless the focus of their pranks is moved, in this case, Matthew. Matthew was therefore sent to stay with relatives, and the actions ceased. However, when Matthew returned, the disturbances started again, only much worse.

Many people thought that it was in fact Matthew who had deliberately deceived his parents, in order to gain more attention from them, but many of the occurrences could not be explained away that easily. For example, one room would suddenly become extremely cold when the rest of the house was warm, and it was proved that Matthew had not interfered with the central heating system.

The most amazing case of poltergeists ever to come to light lasted between August 1977 and September 1978, in a council house in Enfield, just north of London. Practically every type of poltergeist activity happened, with over 1500 separate events recorded between August and March alone. The events started fairly quietly, a shuffling sound which came from the floor of a bedroom, followed by a knocking sound which continued for the full eleven months. Soon after, a deep, crude voice was heard, and even tape-recorded by investigators at the house. Nobody could identify from whom the voice had come; eventually the voice itself claimed to belong to a seventy-two-year-old man who lived around the corner. Naturally enough, when asked about this, the man denied it, and his voice was much lighter in tone anyway.

By now, the house had become full with social workers, a speech therapist, photographers, priests, psychologists and parapsychologists, all of whom were baffled by the events. On one occasion, a toy brick suddenly appeared, and flew across the room, striking one of the photographers on the head. Pieces of cloth suddenly burst into flames. A box of matches lying in a drawer suddenly ignited, then extinguished themselves before setting fire to anything else in the drawer. Various metal objects began to bend and twist out of shape. Eventually, large pieces of furniture, including a chest of drawers, a sofa and a double bed, started to throw themselves around the house.

As so often is the case with poltergeists, the focus of the paranormal activity was a young girl; in this case, Janet, the twelve-year-old daughter. The deep voice mentioned above seemed to issue from her. She was seen by two different witnesses levitating in mid-air, and she and her sister were thrown out of bed in the middle of the night so that they eventually decided to sleep on the floor. Even that did not put an end to the poltergeist's mischief – Janet was found, fast asleep, on top of a radio in her bedroom. When Janet was seized by the force it was very difficult to hold her down. One of the parapsychologists tried to hold her down on one occasion, and had to use his whole weight to prevent her from being raised into the air. Despite the number of experts from many different fields who spent time at the house, no satisfactory explanation of the events has ever been offered, save for the manifestation of a poltergeist. All manner of tests were performed, and nobody could explain what happened at that house in any other way.

Another famous case of poltergeist activity was centred on a military base in Folkestone, Kent, in 1974. Three parapsychologists, accompanied by an obligatory armed guard, were investigating a house on the base, when they all heard the sound of breaking glass behind them. When they turned round, they saw a light bulb gently rocking to and fro on the floor of the landing, and one of the researchers picked it up. The glass was warm, there were no visible cracks, and the filament was intact. What puzzled the researchers was how did the bulb get there in the first place? If it had fallen from one of the light fittings, it would have had to have travelled about 26 feet (8 m) round a corner from the nearest room. Even if, by some freak, it had made such a journey, how did it not break? In the same building, a laundry basket, which was too heavy for three army men to carry, moved itself from the ground floor of the house to the airing cupboard upstairs, very close to where the light bulb had been found. Another time, the table in the dining room had been set for an official function, and two sets of cutlery mysteriously disappeared.

All of the above could, just about, be explained away as a group of pranksters playing with the minds of those affected. This would have been very hard to accomplish, given that the house was on a military base, and under armed guard. Whatever the reason, one thing is for certain: outbreaks of poltergeist activity are too frequent to be brushed off as simply the work of practical jokers. For this reason, researchers have studied the phenomenon closely, to try to explain

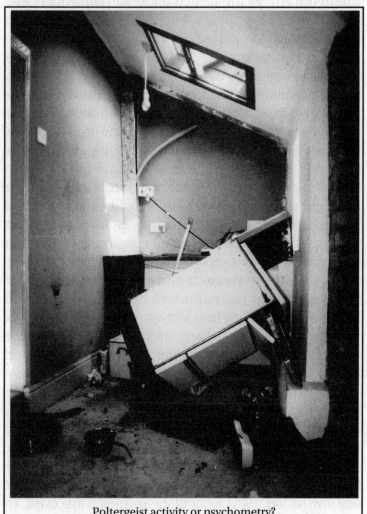

Poltergeist activity or psychometry?

where the energy for alleged poltergeist activity comes from.

One much-supported theory is that poltergeist activity is somehow created by sexual tension. Countless cases have centred around young girls on the threshold of sexual maturity, and the height of the activity is most frequently found in their bedrooms. In the aforementioned case in Enfield, the main victim of the attacks was Janet, the twelve-year-old daughter. In order to strengthen their belief in this theory, many researchers have had to ignore an awful lot of evidence which is contrary to the theory, and in many cases, young girls are not involved in any way. In the last century, the experiences of a very famous psychic, Daniel Dunglas Home, opened discussion about paranormal activity associated with men, but so strong was the view that pubescent girls were the source of poltergeist activity that researchers of the time simply said that Mr Home was an exception because he was a homosexual (which was merely rumoured, never proven).

It is only relatively recently that male victims of poltergeist attacks have been taken seriously. A case in point happened in Glasgow between August 1974 and May 1975. The epicentre of the attacks focused on two boys aged fifteen and eleven who lived with their parents in a tenement flat. They experienced hearing a series of peculiar sounds, followed by strange knocking noises. It turned out, after an investigation, that the most likely explanation for their experiences was that they were telepathically linked with an old gentleman who lived on the ground floor of their building. He was suffering from cancer and, as his condition deteriorated, the knocking which affected the boys grew stronger and more frequent. When he died from his condition, the knocking and the strange noises abruptly stopped.

This case served to strengthen the opinions of those who believed that these visitations are somehow linked to puberty, because of the ages of the boys. However, it would be wrong to assume that this is always the case. Adults long past the age of puberty have had similar experiences, although cases have shown that the person affected has in some way suffered from sexual problems. A typical example of such a situation involved a forty-eight-year-old man from York who lived with his elderly uncle and experienced poltergeist activity. Whenever he entered his uncle's study, the desk moved, chairs scraped across the floor and the windows opened and shut rapidly. This continued for almost three years, until the victim sought medical advice for the mental problems which his experiences had caused. He was found to be impotent and was given treatment. Less than one week after receiving the treatment, the activity abruptly ceased.

One very significant statistic is that, of all recorded cases of poltergeist activity, nearly 90 per cent have been experienced by families who have recently moved house. Any house move is stressful, often accompanied by a change of job or school, leaving friends behind and trying to make new ones – obviously this causes tension to mount within the family. This leads to the second school of thought on the causes of poltergeist activity, namely that poltergeists are not, in fact, mischievous spirits, but the movement of objects is caused by an individual's mind, through the power, reluctant or not, of psychokinesis.

The study of psychokinesis really began in the mid-nineteenth century with the birth of the Spiritualist movement (see Chapter 6). In 1870, two well-respected parapsychologists made a series of twenty-nine controlled tests. One of the experimenters was the medium Daniel Dunglas Home, the other was one of the foremost scientists of the time, William Crookes. Crookes was brought on board as a sceptic, and was soon convinced of Home's ability to move objects using the power of his mind. In his reports, Crookes stated that psychic abilities are closely linked to the state of mind of the subject, and that psychokinesis implied the existence of "inexplicable contact with a plane of existence [in the subject] not his own". Crookes's experiments were to be repeated by many other scientists. Polish medium Stanislawa Tomczyk was carefully studied between 1912 and 1914 by a team of researchers. The studies showed that Stanislawa was able to produce poltergeist-like phenomena spontaneously and at will, including making objects rise into the air without touching them.

Research into the field of psychokinesis really took off in the 1960s, when psychic mediums suddenly began to make themselves available for scientific examination. The most highly regarded of these mediums was the Russian Nina Kulagina, who made herself available for study in 1968. Since then, she has been filmed performing psychokinesis, and there is no evidence that she ever resorted to fraudulent means. British investigator Benson Herbert gave testimony to her skills. He reported that she was able to make objects move either towards or away from her on a table, and even cause three different objects to move in different directions. Amazingly, she was even able to stop the beating of a frog's heart and to give a sceptical observer a heart attack. Benson Herbert reported that during a series of experiments, she placed a hand on his forearm, and he began to feel an unbearable heat. He said after the incident, ". . . if Kulagina had maintained her grip on my arm for half an hour or so, I would have followed the way of the frog".

After devoting his life to the study of the paranormal and psychic phenomena, famous researcher Dr Rhine summed up his feelings on psychokinesis:

> *"It staggers my imagination to conceive all the implications that follow now that it has been shown that the mind, by some means as unknown as the mind itself, has the ability directly to affect material operations in the world around it . . . Mind is what the man in the street thought it was all along – something of a force in itself."*

So is psychokinesis the real culprit responsible for poltergeist activity? Countless years of research, as so often in the field of the paranormal, have proven nothing conclusive. The problem with the psychokinesis theory is that the energy involved in many poltergeist disturbances far exceeds anything shown under test conditions by psychokinetics. The best that these mediums have achieved is the movement of very small objects, whereas poltergeist reports have shown large items of furniture being thrown around the room. In light of this, many researchers have looked for other explanations for poltergeist attacks, but as yet have come up with nothing. What really puzzles the author is: why would any spirit that can show such incredible stores of psychic energy bother using them for such purposeless means? Can't it do something more interesting with its afterlife?

Remote viewing

In recent years, members of the American security services have admitted that they have used astonishing psychic techniques for espionage. Those who came forward decided not to use terminology such as "telepathy", "clairvoyance" or "out of body", but preferred a more scientific-sounding phrase – "remote viewing".

The Pentagon authorized the use of remote viewers for espionage under code names such as "Gondola Wish", "Star Gate" and "Grill Flame". In one operation, remote viewers were asked by the CIA to examine the new US embassy in Moscow, which had been constructed by Soviet workers. The viewers were asked to determine whether or not the building had been bugged, but to do so without visiting the building. In fact, they did their job while remaining in America. They claimed that there were masses of bugs in the building, and that the building had been constructed in such a way that the girders acted as an antenna. All of their findings were confirmed when the building was physically checked out, and the building was pulled down as a result.

In another mission, the remote viewing unit were given a photograph of a building taken by a spy satellite. Their superiors asked them what was being constructed inside the building. The viewers described an enormous submarine, the likes of which had never been seen before. They described its double hull and

175

missile payload in great detail. They even predicted how and when the submarine would be launched. At the time, the American National Security Council dismissed their claims as rubbish, as the "submarine" would have been so big that they could never have believed that the Russians were capable of keeping it secret. A few months later, they had to eat their words when satellite photographs confirmed the existence of the new "Typhoon" class submarine.

No one as yet understands how remote viewing is performed, not even those who have actively practised it. Some believe that it is a form of out-of-body experience, where the psyche detaches from the physical body and is free to roam, reporting back what it has seen. One thing does seem to be certain. It is the intuitive, creative side of the brain that seems most able to perform this activity. The scientific side of the brain does not seem able to cope with how these things happen, and therefore actively prevents them from happening. The remote viewing unit of the US military was staffed in the main by creative, artistic people and, hard though it may be to believe of the military, they were given a free rein, with little scientific observation. The authorities at the time were more interested in the results rather than how those results were achieved, and this worked in their favour.

By 1995, the programme had conducted several hundred intelligence collection projects involving thousands of remote viewing sessions. Over a period of two decades, $20 million was spent on remote viewing activities, and the project is now believed to have been closed down. The remote viewing unit's successes were labelled "eight martini" results, because the data collected was so unbelievable that one has to drink eight martinis in order for the brain to cope! Below is a list of the major successes of the remote viewing unit.

In 1974, one remote viewer correctly described an airfield, which turned out to be a secret Soviet nuclear testing area.

In the same year, a remote viewer was asked to locate a Soviet bomber that had crashed somewhere in Africa. He gave coordinates which enabled the wreckage to be found.

In 1979 the remote viewing unit accurately described the production of the new Soviet "Typhoon" class submarine, including its launch date, all of which was verified by US spy satellites on the day in question.

In 1988, the unit was asked to find Colonel William Higgins, who had been taken hostage by the Lebanese. One viewer stated that Higgins was in a specific building in a named South Lebanon village. Another hostage who was later released declared that on the day in question it was likely that Higgins had indeed been in that very building.

A KGB colonel was arrested in South Africa on a charge of spying. A remote viewer stated that the colonel had been using a pocket calculator which contained a communications device to report back to his superiors. The South African Intelligence unit then used this line of questioning and gained the spy's admission and cooperation.

The remote viewers continued to operate until 1995. In the article in the *Washington Post* on 30 December 1996, one agent from the unit told the newspaper how the unit had been used to see future events immediately prior to the Gulf War. On 15 May 1987, the agent in question turned up for work, and was given some map coordinates to "view" by his superiors. He didn't know that the coordinates did not actually exist on any map – he was being used to detect general phenomena, to pick up on whatever was out there. The agent wrote a nineteen-page stream-of-consciousness report which went into incredible detail, and was so amazing when compared with later events that it was sent straight up the chain of command, possibly even as high as the president himself. The agent described an event involving a US warship. He saw a "bright flash" and then heard a rushing sound, which he said reminded him of an Exocet missile. The event occurred at night, and he described it as feeling almost "unreal – can't believe this is going on". He said that the event involved two different nationalities or races, and that there was a sense of the unexpected about the event. He believed that the damage caused had been done unintentionally.

The following week caused a bit of a stir in the remote viewing unit, in light of the report made by the agent. An Iraqi fighter plane had fired two Exocet missiles at the USS *Stark* which was operating in the Persian Gulf. One of the missiles hit the ship. At the time, America and Iraq were not at war; in fact, the US was secretly aiding Iraq in the war against Iran, so the US accepted the apology from Iraq that the bombing was an accident caused by an inexperienced pilot.

The agent's original nineteen-page document was apparently so detailed in its description of the events which happened to the USS *Stark* that people took notice. Had the agent seen into the future (not by any means the remit of the remote viewing unit, but think of the military implications), or was this just an elaborate coincidence? Unfortunately, this is the only (public) report of any such clairvoyant activity experienced by the unit, and it is believed that no further research into the area has been undertaken by the Pentagon.

The remote viewing unit was wound up in 1995, and the American government has ceased all research into the possible uses of the phenomenon. At least, that is what the public has been told. Military operations are notoriously secretive, and the successes of the remote viewers have in many instances been extremely accurate. I for one would not be in the least surprised if future reports of psychic abilities used for military operations appeared in the press. The possibilities are too great to ignore.

Psychic Healing

. . . .

Mind over body

For centuries, doctors, healers and shamans used a combination of physical and mental (many would say "psychic") medicine to cure their patients. It is only really in the last two centuries that we have lost the mental aspect of healing, giving way to the tremendous advances in medical science. No wonder really – science won the day, proving that through research it could conquer a vast array of illnesses and diseases. Many of the ailments which were previously thought of as fatal have actually been eradicated by scientific techniques such as immunization. Consider tuberculosis, leprosy, scarlet fever, measles, and even the plague.

Doctors in the modern world often overlook the role of the mind in aiding recovery, although they are all too eager to diagnose symptoms as being psychosomatic. So, in short, they are willing to concede that an illness may be the product of the mind, but not willing to accept that the mind is capable of curing an illness. Some doctors are willing to accept that the state of mind of a patient can speed recovery or slow down the onslaught of disease, and there is a lot of evidence to show that sufferers from cancer, for example, survive longer if they believe in their own ability to combat the disease rather than giving in to it. Psychic healers concentrate on this aspect – they help the sick to heal themselves, and provide psychic energy to boost the patient's own self-healing powers. This is by no means a new theory. Shamans have practised the art of healing in this way for centuries.

Shamanism

Shamans, tribal healers, began their form of medicine long before doctors existed, and certainly a long time before hospitals were built. They can be traced back nearly 50,000 years, and still have great influence in many parts of the world. The most basic belief of the shamans is that there are two realities – the reality of the physical world and the reality of the mental/spiritual world. Unlike Western societies, shamans regard the spiritual world as of equal if not greater significance than the physical, and they think of the two worlds as real places which can be travelled between.

For millennia, shamans honed their healing techniques. They became experts on herbs and plants, not only for use in healing, but also to induce altered states of consciousness, thereby increasing their psychic abilities and communication with the astral world. In visions and out-of-body states they are able to receive messages about a person's illness and how to deal with it. The shamans' greatest achievement remains the invention of holistic medicine, based on the idea that the body and mind are one, and directly affect each other.

When the Danish explorer Knud Rasmussen arrived in arctic North America in 1921, his aim was to study the Iglulik Eskimos. He uncovered a culture that centred almost entirely around a host of unseen beings – spirits that lived in every person, animal and object and other spirits that were held responsible for crop growth, illness, bad weather and anything else you may care to mention. Rasmussen was taught the beliefs of the people by an Eskimo shaman named Anarqâq. Rasmussen learned that certain spirits were benevolent and helpful, others malevolent and aggressive, and some just plain evil. Although the entire community of the Eskimos held ceremonies to banish the bad spirits, only the shamans were successful in ridding their people of them completely. As a shaman, Anarqâq was helped by the good spirits who presented themselves to him through possession. While possessed by the spirits, Anarqâq believed that he held their powers to use at his own will and would thus be better equipped to fight off the evil spirits.

Professor Stanley Krippner is one of the world's leading experts on shamanism, and as part of his ongoing research, he has travelled the globe to meet these great healers in their own tribes. One of Krippner's reports details how a shaman was "initiated" into her role by her tribe in southern Africa.

At school, Margaret Umlazi began to have seizures, which were thought to be the result of epilepsy. Instead of trying to gain medical treatment for her seizures, Margaret's tribal elders asked her about her "dream life", and she told them of a recurring dream that she had been having in which she was dragged to the bottom of a lake by a giant serpent. In her dreams, however, everything was all right, as she found that she was able to breathe underwater. Her elders told her that the serpent was one of her ancestors, and that the lake into which she was being dragged represented the astral world. By showing that she could breathe underwater, Margaret had in effect shown that she was able to survive in that other world, and therefore had the makings of a shaman, and she was duly trained to be a tribal healer.

A standard method of healing among shamanic communities is to put the sick person into a trance, which often results in dramatic convulsions. In this state, the patient can release his or her tensions and eradicate unclean spirits. In most cases this actually seems to work. The fact that shamans have an ability to cure is almost without doubt, although whether this ability is brought about through the unique powers which the shaman possesses, or if the secret lies in the mind of the one being healed, who is convinced of the shaman's ability, is a matter for conjecture. If a cure is the result by whatever means, then does it really matter?

The whole concept of shamanism – the herbs that they use, the fusion of their minds with the spirit world, channelling powers from spirit guides – can clearly be seen as the basis for the philosophy behind modern spiritual and psychic healers. Many people today are turning to alternative methods of healing when "conventional" medicine seems to offer them little chance of recovery. However, unlike the shamans, most modern healers consider their craft to be complementary medicine rather than a replacement; it should run alongside the treatment prescribed by a doctor.

Psychic healer, or quack?

Does a psychic healer really possess a tremendous power to cure disease, or is it simply a matter of faith on the part of the patient? The "laying on of hands" is a common practice among faith healers, and if this and other such techniques really do help people to recover from illness, then the medical profession must surely appreciate the significance of what is happening. Alas, the medical profession in general still regards spiritual and psychic healers as "quacks", charlatans who bring a bad name to the business of healing. Many doctors will refer patients for alternative treatment such as homeopathy or chiropractic healing, but to a faith healer? I think not. In fact, faith healers have only very rarely been tested during this century, as most scientists would think that their reputations might be tarnished by such trivial investigation. Dr Bernard Grad, a biochemist from Canada, was one of the few who considered that the ramifications of the laying on of hands were too important to be ignored. He believed that it was a phenomenon that warranted a full investigation, and during the 1950s he set about doing just that.

Grad was spurred on by evidence collected during the trialling of new drugs which had uncovered a marvel called "the placebo effect". When tests are conducted to determine the effects of a new drug, a control group is always used. The control group is given something that looks exactly like the new drug, but is in fact a plain sugar pill. In a good number of such trials, the control group has experienced exactly the same beneficial results as those who took the real drug, and this became known as the placebo effect.

Grad, and many others, believed that this was proof, under laboratory conditions, that the mind, when under a suggestive influence, can directly affect the body, in particular, the healing process.

The placebo effect is not simply limited to the development of new pharmaceutical drugs. Placebo surgery has produced some astounding results. Angina sufferers have been taken into the operating theatre, opened up and then stitched up again, with no actual surgery on the angina itself being performed. A very high percentage of such patients have made quite remarkable recoveries. There is also the concept of the "nocebo", the negative effect placebo. In this case, the proper drugs are administered to a patient, but the patient has little or no faith in their doctor, and they fail to recover from their illness. In the case of both the placebo and nocebo, it would appear that faith and belief play a major part.

Much research was undertaken into the placebo effect, but Grad thought that this research was not far-reaching enough in its remit. He decided to see if he could devise experiments which would qualify the existence of some force between psychic healers and their patients. The main problem that he faced, as a scientist, was how to remove the possibility of suggestion or faith on the part of the subject – in other words, he needed to remove any possibility of a placebo effect happening in his work. Grad concluded that the only way to do this was to work on animals and plants, not humans, for humans would always run the risk of believing that they would be cured. Next, Grad needed an alleged psychic healer, and he chose a retired Hungarian called Oskar Estebany. Estebany had discovered his ability to heal when working with cavalry horses during his years in the army, and in later life had transferred his skills to heal humans. He had never charged for his services, which involved a laying on of hands.

In Grad's first experiment, he removed a small piece of skin under anaesthetic from the backs of forty-eight mice. The mice were then weighed and the size of their wounds was measured and written down. The mice were then divided into three groups of sixteen, and each group was placed in a separate cage. Estebany was to "care" for one of the groups of mice, and his treatment involved standing their cage on his left hand, and resting his right hand on the top. At no stage did he actually touch the mice themselves. The second group received exactly the same feeding routines, but no other intervention – this was the control group. The final group of mice was cared for exactly the same as Estebany's group, but with one exception. Instead of being "treated" by Estebany, the mice were warmed to a temperature equivalent to that generated by Estebany's hands, to determine whether heat alone would accelerate the healing process.

The mice's wounds were measured on a regular basis over a period of twenty days in order to analyse their recovery rate. There was very little difference between the control group and the mice that had been warmed, but the mice treated by Estebany recovered at a far quicker rate. The scars of the mice treated by the healer had shrunk to the size of a pencil point, and most of those on the mice from the other two groups were much larger. Scientists would never accept such evidence as proof of healing ability unless the experiment could be replicated elsewhere. The same experiment was therefore conducted at the

University of Manitoba in Canada, this time using 300 mice. Once again, those mice treated by Estebany showed the most rapid rate of recovery.

Grad firmly believed that he was on the verge of a great scientific discovery, proven under scientific conditions. He decided to continue with his experiments with Estebany, this time using plants. He devised an experiment to see if Estebany could influence the growth and rate of germination of barley seeds. The only difference this time between the control group and Estebany's group was that Estebany held the watering can for his group. The vast majority of those in Estebany's group grew far quicker and healthier than the control group. Grad summed up what he believed the experiment proved:

> "Something must have passed from [Estebany's] hand to the solution which was then delivered to the seeds. And since the treatment in most of the experiments was through the barrier of a sealed glass container, it cannot be a material substance in a sense that it is a chemical of any kind. I know of no other way to explain these experiments, and so I am inclined to feel that there was something from the hand that was being radiated and this penetrated the glass bottle and went in and altered the water."

In other words, Grad believed that Estebany had somehow channelled energy into the solution, providing it with healing powers. In effect, Estebany had channelled healing energy.

The results of Grad's experiments have led many scientists to question and research the possibility of psychic healing, and several have reported findings which corroborate his evidence. However, as far as psychic healing goes, we still cannot explain how the process is achieved. Whether or not something actually passes from the healer to the patient is still debatable – people still question whether or not it is simply a matter of faith, though how Grad's seedlings could have believed in the healing capabilities of Estebany is a bigger mystery to me than anything else. One thing is for certain. Psychic healing, however it works, can and does work. I would never suggest that it should replace modern medicine, but it has brought hope and even cures to those whom medical science had written off as incurable.

Psychic surgery

Can the power of the mind replace the scalpel in the operating room? The knee-jerk response to such a question is obviously, "no way". Psychic surgery is the term given to the practice of paranormal surgery using only bare hands or very simple instruments. The theory goes that the psychic surgeon's hands enter the patient's body, seemingly without scarring, and the result is a cure of the patient's ailment. Is this another case of the "placebo effect", the patient fully believing in the psychic surgeon's powers and thus, in effect, their mind cures their own body? Or do those who claim to have the ability really possess a power beyond our imagination?

One such psychic surgeon was the Brazilian Jose Pedro De Freitas, who became known throughout the world simply as "Arigo". Arigo first discovered his talent when he was sitting with friends, gathered around the bed of a dying woman. A priest had arrived to give the woman, who was near death due to an inoperable tumour in her uterus, the last rites. Her death was expected at any moment. Suddenly, unaware of what he was doing, Arigo dashed from the room, returning with a kitchen knife. He ordered everyone to stand back, then plunged the knife into the woman's vagina and twisted it several times. He inserted his hand, pulled out a huge tumour, the size of a grapefruit, then fell back into a chair and began to cry. The grieving relatives and friends stood in shock, and a doctor was called to the scene, but the patient had felt no pain whatsoever. When the doctor arrived, he confirmed that Arigo had removed the tumour, and that the woman was not even bleeding. She recovered her health completely.

Arigo suddenly found himself in great demand from people who had been diagnosed as incurable although he had no memory of his "operation" on the woman. His amazing surgery soon became a daily event in his home town, and it became apparent that he was performing his cures while in a trance-like state. Also, his patients noticed that he spoke in a German accent when in this trance, allegedly because he was under the guidance and control of Dr Adolphus Fritz, a German doctor who had died in 1918. On any one day, Arigo would arrive at his "surgery" to find over 200 people queuing for his services. His methods were crude and brutal; he would push people against a wall, and jab them with an unsterilized knife which he would then wipe on his shirt before his next "operation". Startlingly, his patients felt neither pain nor fear – there was little or no blood, and the wound, where he had stabbed them with his penknife, would heal completely in a matter of days.

During the 1950s and 1960s, Arigo became a national hero in Brazil, and he performed an estimated 500,000 operations over a five-year period, without ever accepting a single payment for his services. As his fame grew, a researcher from New York, Andrija Puharich, paid him a visit, together with a team of doctors. Puharich described what he saw as like a scene from a nightmare:

> "These people step up – they're all sick. One had a big goitre. Arigo just picked up the paring knife, cut it open, popped the goitre out, slapped it in her hand, wiped the opening with a piece of dirty cotton, and off she went. It hardly bled at all."

Puharich even tested Arigo's abilities first hand. He asked Arigo to remove a benign tumour from his arm, which Arigo did in a matter of seconds, using only a knife. Arigo never had a single allegation brought against him by a patient that his surgery had done any harm, yet he was twice imprisoned for his activities. On the first occasion, the Brazilian president gave Arigo a pardon, but on the second occasion, that president was no longer in power, and he served seven months in jail. On both occasions, however, the prison wardens let him out of his cell to perform operations on the sick.

The judge at Arigo's appeal hearing, Filippe Immesi, decided that the only way that he could properly make a decision on the case was to study Arigo's techniques for himself. A near-blind woman, with cataracts on both eyes, had visited Arigo for help on the day that the judge came to inspect his work. Arigo asked the judge to hold the woman's head while he performed his operation. The judge had the following to say after witnessing the amazing event:

> *"I saw him pick up what looked like a pair of nail scissors. He wiped them on his sport shirt, and used no disinfectant of any kind. Then I saw him cut straight into the cornea of the patient's eye. She did not blench, although she was fully conscious. The cataract was out in a matter of seconds. The district attorney and I were speechless, amazed. Then Arigo said some kind of prayer as he held a piece of cotton in his hand. A few drops of liquid suddenly appeared on the cotton and he wiped the woman's eye with it. We saw this at close range. She was cured."*

The judge was convinced that Arigo was a genuine man with a unique gift, but what he was doing remained illegal. Immesi did all he could to reduce Arigo's sentence, and sent him back to prison for only two months. During the trial, the judge listened to evidence given by the mainstream medical profession, who were worried particularly by the prescriptions that Arigo had given to many of his patients. Dr Ary Lex, a distinguished surgeon, witnessed four of Arigo's operations, and was satisfied that what Arigo was doing was a paranormal phenomenon, but he took offence at the drugs that Arigo prescribed his patients, more often than not without even looking at them. He described some of the drugs as extremely dangerous in the doses which Arigo prescribed, and testified that "They were absolutely ridiculous. Some of them were for obsolete medicines which were only still being made because *he* prescribed them."

So, in the expert opinion of the medical profession, Arigo's prescriptions were absurd. But they worked. Always. In one instance, a Polish lady who was riddled with cancer visited Arigo as a last resort. Her cancer had been discovered when she visited a clinic complaining of an intestinal blockage, and it was found that the blockage was a malignant tumour. She had to have a colostomy, but the cancer spread remorselessly. When she visited Arigo, he glanced at her and wrote out a prescription, saying, "You take this, you get well." Her doctor administered the drugs, against his better judgment, for the dosage was absurd. She showed signs of improvement after just one week, and after six weeks she returned to visit Arigo, who gave her two more prescriptions. On her third visit, Arigo announced that she was completely cured, and that she should have her colostomy operation reversed. She duly made arrangements with a surgeon, and when her abdomen was opened the surgeons confirmed that all signs of her cancer had vanished completely.

Arigo himself had no explanation for his gift, and more often than not was completely unaware of what he was doing. Was he being controlled by the spirit of a dead German doctor? We shall never know, for Arigo died in 1971. Arigo only gave thanks to Christ and to Doctor Fritz – that is all that we know. His methods were bizarre – he even fainted when he saw a video of himself performing his psychic surgery – but it is beyond doubt that they helped to cure hundreds of thousands of people when the medical profession had written them off.

Psychic healers today

The ability of certain individuals to heal by unconventional methods is becoming more accepted throughout the world. In Britain, it is now possible to gain treatment from psychic healers in exceptional circumstances through the National Health Service. However, the more extravagant claims made by healers are still regarded by the medical profession with scorn.

One such healer who uses hypnotherapy as the main conduit for his healing claimed that his techniques enabled one of his patients to regrow part of her foot which was lost in an accident. Joe Keeton is the mystic in question, and when ridiculed by the medical community, he simply points to the woman and shows them her foot – irrefutable evidence of his amazing ability. Keeton uses hypnosis to channel visualization which he claims enables the body to heal itself dramatically. He argues that there is a universal field of energy which directs the creation of the body from the DNA in individual cells, and it is possible to enable the mind to kick this energy into action, restoring sick parts of the body.

Rather than simply let modern healers practise their art, scientists are obsessed with testing their abilities under laboratory conditions. Carol Everett, a psychic healer from England, participated in a series of tests at Denki University in Tokyo. Carol was introduced to a young woman whom she had never met before, and was asked to detect her illness by psychic means alone. Carol herself was hooked up to a variety of monitoring machines to measure her heart rate, brain activity, blood pressure and respiration rate.

Carol diagnosed that the young woman had ovarian cancer, which the doctors present confirmed to be true. Carol then began to administer her healing powers to the young woman, all the while being monitored by the scientists' machinery. As the healing process continued, the machines registered that the left hemisphere of Carol's brain had almost completely shut down, and the right hemisphere was working at an exceptional rate. The right hemisphere of the brain is associated with the creative and psychic side of the human personality. The left hemisphere is associated with the scientific, mathematical and rational processes. Carol was also displaying alpha brain wave activity, which usually only registers during sleep.

The results from the machinery monitoring Carol paled into insignificance when compared with the machine that was monitoring her patient. A scanner was hooked up to the young woman, showing a clear picture of her ovarian tumour. As the healing process continued, the tumour was shown to cool and shrink, until, after about seven minutes, it vanished altogether. At this point, Carol emerged from her trance and announced that the healing process was complete. Tests on her patient showed that she had been completely cured. Finally a psychic had performed a complete healing procedure under laboratory conditions, and multi-million-pound technology had confirmed her powers as documented fact.

Reiki

Reiki is a form of psychic healing developed in Japan. The word *Reiki* is a Japanese word meaning "universal life-force energy", and it is a system of channelling that energy to someone for the purpose of healing. It was discovered, according to most records, by Dr Mikao Usui in the late nineteenth century. Usui was a Christian minister in Japan, and made it his mission in life to discover the way in which Jesus had healed the sick. He studied at theological colleges in America, but found no answers, and tried to find out by reading Buddhist writings, but all to no avail. After several years of study, he felt that he had come to a basic understanding of the principles of healing, and that to go further required in-depth meditation. He declared to the monks of his monastery his intention to fast and meditate for twenty-one days on a nearby mountain, and that if he did not return after that time, they should come to recover his body.

He went to the mountain and collected twenty-one stones with which to count the days. As each day passed, he would throw one of the stones away. On the night of the twentieth day, he threw away the final stone, having discovered absolutely nothing. During the night, he saw a ball of light on the horizon, slowly approaching him. As it got closer, his first instinct was to run away, but he realized that this might just have been what he was waiting for, so he sat there while the light got closer, and eventually hit him square on the forehead. As the light struck him, he was taken on a mystical journey, and shown bubbles of all the colours of the rainbow enclosing the symbols of Reiki. When Usui returned from the mountain, he found that he had an incredible power to heal. On his first day back at the monastery, he healed the broken toenail of a monk, an ailing tooth, his own starvation, and the abbot's sickness which had kept him bedridden for months. These have become known as the first four miracles of Reiki.

Usui wanted to use his new-found abilities to help others, and spent the next seven years in the poorest area of Tokyo, healing the sick, and helping the poor to improve their lives. At the end of this seven years, he started to notice familiar faces, those of people whom he'd healed years before and who had returned to the impoverished area. When he asked them why they had returned, they complained that life outside the slums was too hard, and that it was much simpler to beg for a living. In Usui's mind, they had thrown away the gift of health as if it had no value.

Usui returned to the monastery. He had realized that he had not taught gratitude along with the healing, that he had merely focused on the physical illnesses without dealing with the spiritual side of things. The people he had treated did not understand the value of what he had given them. After some time meditating in the monastery, he decided to travel around the countryside, from village to village, teaching both physical and spiritual healing.

During these travels, he met Dr Chujiro Hayashi, a naval commander. Hayashi was very impressed with the conviction and sincerity of Usui, and asked to accompany him on his travels. After Usui passed on, Hayashi took over his work, opening a clinic in Tokyo, near the Imperial Palace. The clinic consisted of eight beds in a large room, with two Reiki practitioners per patient. One would treat the head, the other would treat the stomach area, then both would treat the patient's back. Dr Hayashi developed what is now the most common form of Reiki, a type of treatment using specific hand placements over the body.

Hayashi committed suicide in 1940, shortly before Japan attacked Pearl Harbor. As a reserve officer, Dr Hayashi knew that he would be called to duty and would therefore become responsible for killing many people. He could not live with this thought, and so ended his own life. Before he did so, he passed on the Reiki teachings to Mrs Hawayo Takata.

Mrs Takata was born in Hawaii, of Japanese descent. During the 1930s, she went to Japan to visit her family, and while there, she became very sick, and needed an urgent operation. When she was in hospital, she kept hearing voices in her head telling her "operation not necessary". Just as she was about to receive the anaesthetic, she jumped off the bed and asked if there was some other way to cure her that did not involve an operation. The surgeon had a sister who had been cured of dysentery at Dr Hayashi's clinic, and he referred Mrs Takata there. After her treatment at Dr Hayashi's clinic, Mrs Takata persuaded Dr Hayashi to train her in Reiki. Takata was eventually trained as a Reiki master, and took over Dr Hayashi's work upon his death.

Mrs Takata has widely promoted Reiki throughout the world, and it is now one of the more widely known forms of healing through direct application of *Chi* – the underlying force that the Chinese believe makes up the universe. Reiki applies an energy quality commonly known as "vibration", and is very simply performed. A practitioner simply places his or her hands upon the person to be healed with the intent for the healing to occur, and then the energy begins to flow. Practitioners believe that this energy form has its own intelligence and knows where it should go within the body in order for the healing to take place.

Nonetheless, there is a prescribed set of hand positions traditionally taught which give good coverage over the recipient's entire body.

The latest development in Reiki techniques is the most psychic of them all. The laying on of hands is one thing, but practitioners are now claiming the ability to perform "remote healings". To the world of the spirit there is no such thing as time or space. The world we see around us is only a small fragment of all which exists. Since there is no time and space to limit spirit, Reiki practitioners believe that they can operate without regard to limitations of space, and that they can bring healing to a patient regardless of distance. In doing remote healings, the recipient is objectified in some way, by using an object (for example a teddy bear) to represent the body of the patient. The practitioner will then practise the Reiki on the object, and the patient, who could be anywhere in the world, receives the healing powers bestowed upon it. There are now many sites on the worldwide web which cater for this practice.

Many people feel that they have been magically healed from all kinds of illnesses by this process. Whether this is an example of mind over matter, the placebo effect or some greater power at work is the subject of debate. But surely what really matters is the end result, that the healing process has been accelerated in one form or another. The statistics show that the mind does have an influence over the body. Belief is a powerful healing tool.

Psychic healing is slowly being accepted by the public as a perfectly legitimate alternative to conventional medicine. In a survey undertaken in 1998, 40 per cent of the British population were found to believe that psychic healing would be useful in the event of a serious illness. This may not sound dramatically high, but it is a full 5 per cent higher than the 35 per cent who expressed a similar belief in the National Health Service.

The Mind Under the Microscope

●●●●●●●●●●●●●●●●●●●●●●●●●●●●●●●●

Scientific testing

There has always been a certain amount of tension between believers in psychic ability and the sceptics. The greatest obstacle to acceptance of paranormal events is not lack of evidence, but the firmly entrenched belief that such events are impossible. The rationalist/spiritualist debate has existed for centuries, and both sides of the argument will claim that they have conclusive evidence to support their views. Perhaps the healthiest result of this ongoing debate has been the willingness of scientists to test theories that go against all scientific thinking, albeit often in an effort to debunk the psychic, but in many cases with some (for them) rather surprising outcomes.

The debate became intense during the nineteenth century. Scientists equated psychical research with Spiritualism, a movement which took off in the middle of the century. Spiritualism in turn was equated with the occult, and occult meant black magic which was linked to witchcraft, considered by scientists to be a remnant from the superstitious Dark Ages from which science had rescued mankind. In the second half of the century, scientists looked back in horror at the cruelties imposed on people by the persecution of so-called "witches". During the hysteria which swept through Europe and America, it is estimated that a quarter of a million people suffered torture and painful death at the hands of those who thought them to be witches. The new scientific revolution led to a new way of thinking. Belief in witchcraft fell out of favour – science had proven it to be folly.

Science replaced religion in many ways as the master of the universe. Technology began to tame the planet. The belief in the impossibility of psychic phenomena largely came about because of the success of the scientific movement. Through science, we came to understand a vast range of natural phenomena, learned how to control heat, light and electricity, and build ships, factories and trains. Humankind was also beginning to be understood as physiologists and neurologists expanded their knowledge. The whole concept of the soul came into question – many intellectuals began to dismiss the idea of such an outmoded notion. What possible place could the concepts of telepathy, clairvoyance, psychokinesis and precognition have in this new scientific world? And what of séances, mediums entering into trances and communicating with the spirit world? According to science and its scientists, these things were simply impossible, and they either ignored them completely or dismissed them as frauds. As far as science was concerned, paranormal phenomena tend not to happen in laboratories, therefore they never happen at all.

It is now widely thought that the scientists of the nineteenth century were wrong to dismiss parapsychology as the food for human gullibility. Of all the sciences, that of parapsychology has the most far-reaching implications for humankind yet, since its humble beginnings in the 1930s, it has been ridiculed by scientists from other fields. It is still not recognized as a true science, and those who choose to research psychic phenomena are generally forced to do so through studying psychology, or to conduct their investigations as a sideline activity, through such organizations as the Society for Psychical Research.

In the 1930s, one man re-ignited interest in the field of parapsychological research. William McDougal was a British physician and psychologist who emigrated to America, where he took the post of Head of Psychology at Harvard University. McDougal was well respected in his fields, and was allowed to devise his own curriculum with his own budgets. Spurred on by his own interest in the paranormal, McDougal used some of the Harvard funds to launch the careers of a number of his students. These included Gardner Murphy, who tried to send mental images to a fellow researcher in Paris and, most importantly, Joseph Banks Rhine, the man who is now credited as being the father of modern parapsychology.

Rhine was at first a renowned sceptic before he read a book by Sir Oliver Lodge, *The Survival of Man*, in which Lodge claimed to have communicated with his dead son through a medium. Lodge was a well-known and much respected physician, and here he was, publishing a book about life after death. The book advocated a full study into psychic capabilities, as without such study, the picture of human nature would be incomplete. On the strength of this, Rhine openly declared that "it would be unpardonable for the scientific world today to overlook evidences of the supernormal in the world – if there are such".

In 1926, Rhine was invited to witness a séance, during which a medium would summon up the spirit of her dead brother, Walter. Rhine was seated next to the medium. When the lights were dimmed and the medium fell into a trance, those present witnessed the playing of music, bells ringing, and the ghost of Walter talking to them. But Rhine was dubious and he watched the medium very closely. Rhine discovered that the medium was a complete fake, and wrote to the American Society for Psychical Research, telling them so. However, the result of his letter was that he became alienated from that society and its British equivalent.

Undeterred, Rhine decided to test psychical abilities under controlled conditions. Back under the wing of his former mentor, William McDougall, Rhine joined his teacher in a new department at Duke University in North Carolina. One of Rhine's colleagues at the university was Karl Zener, an expert in the psychology of perception. Rhine asked Zener to develop a set of five cards, each with an unambiguous design on it. Zener produced a set that contained a circle, a square, a star, a plus sign and a wavy line, and the set has been called "Zener cards" ever since. Rhine's method using the Zener cards was very simple. He had a pack of twenty-five cards, five of each design, and in a test, guesswork would decree that any person should statistically get five correct. Rhine tested many subjects with the cards, mainly with results which mirrored the law of averages. In 1932, Rhine tested one man whom he believed was a genuine psychic, Hubert Pearce.

Over a series of tests, Pearce consistently scored more than double the expected average. On one occasion, Rhine designed an experiment with his assistant, Joseph Pratt. Pearce was told to sit in the university library, while Pratt sat in the physics building, 100 yards (91 m) away. The two men had synchronized their watches, and at a prearranged time, Pratt picked the top card off a deck of Zener cards and placed it face down on the table, without looking at it. He would leave it there for a full minute while Pearce wrote down what he believed it to be, then Pratt would pick up another card. At the end of the session, the two of them would seal their results and hand them to Rhine.

Amazingly, Pearce scored just as highly on these tests as before, suggesting that psychic ability was not limited by distance. This experiment is now considered as the foundation of the phenomenon of remote viewing, used covertly by the American military during the Cold War. Rhine could not explain how this was possible, but did find out that the subject's frame of mind affected their psychic abilities. He discovered that subjects did better when challenged. On one occasion, while testing Pearce, Rhine said that he would give him $100 every time he got one right. Pearce won $2,500 – he got the entire pack right, at staggering odds of 298,023,223,876,953,125 to 1.

After three years of research, and 100,000 tests, Rhine published his results in a monograph, which he entitled "Extrasensory Perception", coining a phrase that is now part of the language. The publication won great acclaim, and became highly controversial. Rhine was accused of fraud, of fiddling his statistics and of conducting poorly controlled experiments. The main criticism of Rhine's work was that it proved to be impossible to repeat, and in all areas of science, results of experiments are considered dubious unless other independent scientists can repeat them. There *were* flaws in Rhine's methods. For example, it would have been possible that a tester could unconsciously move whenever he held up a circle card. His tests may not have been performed under strictly clinical scientific circumstances, but his work made people open to the idea of psychic ability once again, and led to a flood of research in the field.

Following Uri Geller's appearances on television in the 1970s, many tests were made on those who claimed to be able to bend metal using only the power of their minds, and psychokinetic metal bending became a field of study in its own right. Geller himself (who shall be looked at in detail in Chapter 12) took part in supervised experiments in seventeen different scientific laboratories.

The first scientist to perform a thorough enquiry into the phenomenon was Professor Hasted, head of the physics department at Birkbeck College, London. He carried out a series of tests, mainly on children who claimed to have the ability, which he performed both in laboratories and in the children's homes. Although he introduced a more clinical, scientific method of testing, Hasted found that results were improved if the psychological atmosphere of the laboratory was made as comfortable as possible. In an article for *Nature* magazine he stated that "psychokinetic phenomena cannot in general be produced unless all who participate are in a relaxed state". However, the possibility of fraud still had to be removed, so Hasted created experiments in which the metal objects were attached to a strain gauge and a chart recorder. Three of his subjects were able to produce stress signals on the

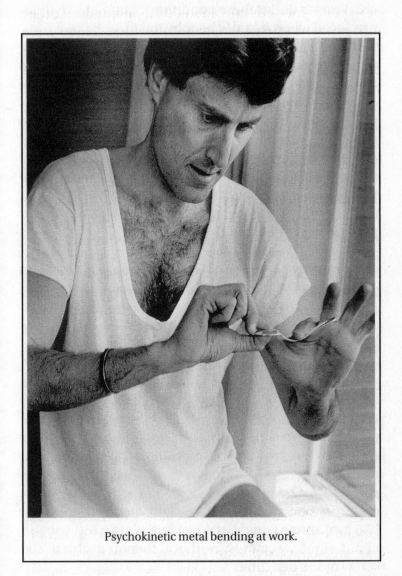

Psychokinetic metal bending at work.

chart paper under these conditions, quite unlike those produced when metal is bent by touch.

Hasted then set about creating tests that under normal circumstances would have been impossible to achieve even by physical means. He placed a handful of straightened paperclips into a glass ball, which was then sealed, and asked his subjects to scrunch the paperclips together. The results were startling – several of Professor Hasted's subjects managed successfully to scrunch the paperclips together while they were inside the sealed glass ball. In December 1976, Professor Hasted published a report in the *Journal of the Society for Psychical Research*. He stated:

> *"I therefore report my belief that I have been able to validate the metal bending phenomenon on a number of occasions by visual witnessing, chart-recording, 'impossible tasks' and the bending of brittle metals."*

Experiments to validate psychokinetic metal bending were taking place all over the world, mostly confirming what Professor Hasted had hypothesized. One very famous metal bender, Jean Pierre Girard, was tested extensively by scientists in France. Girard had claimed that he developed many psychic abilities shortly after he was struck by lightning when he was a child. In one famous experiment, he bent a 3-inch (7.6 cm) screw which was inside a plastic test tube in about fifteen seconds, without touching either the screw or the test tube.

During the 1970s, more and more evidence mounted up from all over the world that the phenomenon of psychokinetic metal bending existed and could be proven. The scientific community could no longer hide from the weight of such confirmed and repeated testing, and at a conference on "Frontiers of Physics" held in Iceland in 1977, it finally became clear that the scientific community had accepted that the human mind was a potential influence on physical processes.

Testing an individual's psychic ability to bend metal or alter physical objects is one thing, and from a scientific point of view, fairly easy to test. But how can scientific testing be applied to the psychic phenomenon of precognition? Most premonitions are too vague to be subjected to scientific study, and in the vast majority of cases, people only mention that they have foreseen an event after the event itself has actually occurred. Statistical studies have shown that planes that crash have fewer people on them than those that do not crash – is this an example of precognition? Or is it just that many planes crash due to bad weather, weather which may have put passengers off flying in the first place? Premonitions such as not taking a flight because of a bad feeling about it cannot be studied. A premonition can only reasonably be tested if it is specific enough to identify a particular incident or individual rather than a general feeling, and then only if the premonition has been notified before the event has taken place.

Timeslips

The whole concept of precognition is one that the scientific community, and many outside the field of science, view with distrust and even contempt. According to the laws of physics, it is an impossibility that anyone can pick up an impression of something which has not yet happened. Time is, after all, a one-way street into the future, it is linear, travelling only forward. Or is it? Much research has been conducted into "timeslips", a strange occurrence which happens when our normal perception of linear time becomes somehow distorted, which can mean experiencing the past as if it were happening now or becoming aware of future events before they happen.

Many questions need to be asked about a precognition when someone experiences one. Most premonitions throughout history have been auguries of disasters. How, then, do we approach testing a premonition? Should we take a fatalistic view, that the future is already mapped out for us and there is nothing that we can do to change it, even if we have foreseen it? If this view was taken, then there would be no point in trying to avert a disaster, as it is pre-ordained. Imagine that I foresee an event very clearly, where a friend of mine is run over by a bright yellow car outside Sainsbury's. Soon afterwards, I am outside Sainsbury's with my friend and the memory of the precognition comes back to me. My friend is wearing exactly the same clothes he was wearing in my vision, and I see a bright yellow car approaching. So, I pull my friend into the shop, away from the danger. What then of my premonition? Did I foresee the future and change it, my vision saving my friend's life? Or, because the event was unfulfilled, was the vision wrong?

Paranormal researchers have tended to approach the study of precognition in a curious way, feeling a need to apply scientific methods to prove its existence. So, if someone claims to have the ability to see into the future, they will be put in front of a random-number generator and asked to predict a six-figure sequence. This has been done many times, with no real proof either way. Understandably so, as in the vast majority of cases, premonitions are not done to order – they just happen spontaneously, without concentration on the part of the supposed psychic.

One man came up with a rather ingenious way of proving his abilities. Dave Mandell had for a long time claimed that he had visions of the future, and had met with a good deal of scepticism as a result. Now, every time that he experiences a premonition, he draws a sketch of what he has seen, then photographs himself holding the sketch in front of a building which has a digital clock displaying the time and the date. He then logs the photograph with witnesses to prove when he had his precognition.

The experience of two ladies on holiday in France in the early twentieth century has been the focus of investigation into the possibility of timeslips for almost a century. The two ladies in question were highly educated rationalists: Miss Anne Moberley was the principal at St Hugh's College, Oxford, and Miss Eleanor Jourdain was head of a girls' school in Watford.

The two ladies visited the Palace of Versailles and had got lost while walking in the gardens, when Miss Moberley noticed a woman shaking a white cloth out of the window of a building. Miss Jourdain saw neither the woman nor the building. They turned a corner, walked past some more buildings, and saw two men at work with a kind of wheelbarrow. Naturally, the two ladies thought nothing of the men whom they assumed to be gardeners, except that their clothing was a little unusual; they were both wearing small, three-cornered hats and long greyish-green coats. The two men gave the ladies directions, which they duly followed.

About this time, they both began to feel depressed, and to notice a curious aspect to their surroundings, which they both believed had become two-dimensional. These feelings grew as they approached a bandstand by which a man was sitting. His face was repulsive and dirty, and he was wearing clothes which looked like they had come from an earlier time. Then they heard footsteps behind them, but when they turned round, the path was empty. Miss Moberley noticed a man standing nearby who seemed to just appear out of thin air. He was tall with curly black hair, and was wearing the same costume as the man by the bandstand. He smiled at the ladies, and then disappeared. As they walked on down the path, Miss Moberley saw a lady sitting on the grass, sketching. The lady looked the two women full in the face, but they passed her without speaking. Miss Moberley turned round, saw the woman again and mentioned it to Miss Jourdain, who commented that she had not seen the lady at all.

A week later, Miss Moberley was still worried about all the strange events in the gardens, and she asked Miss Jourdain if she thought the gardens were haunted. Only now did they explain to each other what they thought had happened on that day, and their accounts differed dramatically. They had both experienced the strange shape that the landscape had taken on, but Miss Moberley had seen far more people than Miss Jourdain had, even though they had both walked past all the "people" mentioned above.

The two ladies were absolutely mystified by their experiences, and decided to pay another visit to Versailles to check their facts out. They discovered that the gardens were completely different from how they remembered them; woods had disappeared, paths had been moved, walls were no longer there and many buildings had vanished. Over the next few years, the two women checked out the history of the gardens and their layout. They discovered that what they had actually walked through on that day were the gardens as they had appeared in the eighteenth century, designed by the French queen's (Marie Antoinette) head gardener.

This case has been the subject of much debate and scrutiny ever since the two ladies made public their experiences. Some have said that they simply made the whole thing up, though quite what their motivation for this would have been, I don't begin to understand. Others have said that they were gullible, elderly spinsters whose heads were filled with romantic nonsense. Still others said that they were subject to a large-scale hallucination caused by a retrospective timeslip.

Experts have looked closely at the case to discern whether or not their experience was paranormal. The fact is that Moberley and Jourdain both had some background knowledge of eighteenth-century French history and of Marie Antoinette's life at Versailles.

However, their visit to the palace was motivated purely by the prospect of a pleasant walk in the gardens; as soon as they first had their experiences, this pleasure was marred, and they became depressed and disorientated. Their written accounts of what happened are quite straightforward, and neither dwell on the supernatural nor go into elaborate historical detail – had they wished to commit a fraud, then their story would probably have included considerably more of both. Many critics have said that the two women had simply seen twentieth-century figures and mistaken them for those of the eighteenth century; but this does in no way explain the changes to the gardens themselves. How could the people have been contemporary if the gardens were not?

The presence of people from another age, the change in the landscape and the exchanges that the two women had with the people they met on their walk through the gardens, all indicate that for Miss Moberley and Miss Jourdain time had become dislocated. The countless interviews and tests that the scientific community undertook to discredit or authenticate the case have only proven one thing: that it is not possible to prove beyond doubt that an experience that revives past events is a paranormal one. Even if there is more than one witness, sceptics will always argue that it was not a real experience, merely an hallucination.

If timeslips do indeed exist, they would explain a multitude of psychic powers and paranormal occurrences. Prophecy, precognition, premonition – whatever we choose to call the ability to foresee future events – all could be explained by the concept of time travelling in two directions. Ghosts and poltergeists could simply be the "memories" of past events playing like a stuck record. Timeslips are one explanation for all of this, but one that the scientific thinkers who believe in the unshakeable concept of linear time could never agree to.

Kirlian photography

For centuries people have believed that psychic ability, the power of the mind, is inextricably connected with the existence of the soul. Since the beginning of time, scientists and mystics alike have pondered the existence of a spiritual body which exists separately from the physical body. In 1970, Russian scientists claimed to have photographed the soul itself.

In 1939, a Russian engineer by the name of Semyon Kirlian received an electric shock while repairing a machine in a research laboratory. He saw a bright flash given off by a spark of electricity, and wondered what would happen if he placed a sheet of light-sensitive paper in the path of the spark. Placing his hand behind such a piece of paper, he found, when he developed the film, strange emanations surrounding each of his fingertips. Over the next forty years, Kirlian devoted his life to researching high-voltage photography, which he believed could discern the aura of the human soul. Some of his most amazing discoveries were made by pure chance. On one occasion, Kirlian was asked to take the "photograph" of a high-ranking Russian official. The photograph showed no sign of any aura, so Kirlian decided to test his wife, to ensure that the machine was working properly. A perfect image was produced. The official developed symptoms of a very virulent influenza the next day, and Kirlian became convinced that his spirit did not show up on film because of the illness. This looked even more likely when, shortly afterwards, Kirlian was visited by the chairman of a major research company, who brought with him two apparently identical leaves to be photographed. The leaves had been taken from the same species of plant, at the same time. Only one leaf showed an aura, and when Kirlian told his visitor, he was delighted, for one of the leaves had been taken from a plant with a serious disease.

Kirlian photography has since been used to detect cancer, which has a very negative effect on the aura. Despite its beneficial results, however, Kirlian photography is still a very controversial tool. The greatest controversy surrounding it is, of course, the interpretation of the results. The first interpretation is held by the sternest of sceptics. They believe any accurate diagnosis of disease is purely coincidental and is based on the intuition of the researcher. Other less sceptical groups believe that the photography picks up physical symptoms such as body temperature and sweat levels, and that poor results are a result of the body reacting to disease in the normal way.

Parapsychologists claim that Kirlian photography can only be fully understood if the existence of an "aura" or some other paranormal phenomenon is considered. Spiritualists believe that Kirlian photography is proof-positive of the existence of the soul – the strange colours and shapes surrounding living objects captured on film is proof of what mystics have been attesting to since the beginning of time.

Whatever the real interpretation, all sides agree that there seems to be a flow of energy surrounding almost all living things. Quite what that energy is remains, for now, a mystery.

Psychometry

The psychic power of psychometrists is another area of the paranormal that has been rigorously tested throughout the years. The word "psychometry", if translated literally from the Greek, means "measuring the soul", and this interpretation is shared by many psychometrists, who believe that they are sensing the soul of a person who has left their mark on an object that they have touched. Psychometrists work by touching objects and receiving impressions of the history either of the object itself, or of those who owned or touched the object.

Professor Joseph Rodes Buchanan, a scientist at the Covington Medical Institute in America, conducted the earliest recorded research into psychometry in the 1840s. Buchanan discovered that some people had the remarkable ability to divine what chemicals were contained within a glass test tube just by holding it. Some of his students could also detect different substances when they were wrapped up in brown paper. Buchanan concluded that the nervous system produced some kind of field, which he called the "nerve aura", which flows from the fingertips and operates like a sixth sense.

What really stunned Buchanan was that some of his

colleagues could hold a sealed letter and accurately describe the person who had written it, and even tell Buchanan the writer's emotional state of mind when they wrote the letter. William Denton, a geologist at the University of Boston and friend of Buchanan, took the research even further. He wrapped three different objects in paper, and handed each of them to one of Buchanan's subjects. The sensitive, on holding the first object, described an island in the midst of blue seas and an erupting volcano. When he held the second object, he explained that he saw it frozen in deep ice, and on holding the third object, described a picture of the universe with glittering stars. Denton was incredibly excited – the first object was a piece of Hawaiian volcanic rock; the second a pebble of limestone from a glacier; the third was a fragment from a meteor.

Buchanan and Denton called this strange ability "psychometry", and the scientific world became very excited about it for a few years, until the arrival of new scientific theories, postulated most notably by Charles Darwin and T. E. Huxley, provoked new scepticism among scientists. Very little research was done into psychometry for the next 120 years, until the arrival on the scene of Tom Lethbridge, a well-known British researcher of the paranormal.

Lethbridge was a well-respected archaeologist, scientist and sceptic of the paranormal. His scepticism was called into question by his neighbour, a psychic who claimed to have the power to leave her body at night and wander around the district. Lethbridge was naturally curious but unconvinced by her claim, until one day his neighbour explained to him how she managed to keep unwanted visitors from her house. What she did was mentally to draw a pentagram and then visualize it across the path of her unwanted visitor, and this would prevent the visitor from entering. Lethbridge dismissed this as hokum, but for amusement one night he imagined drawing pentagrams in his own head and placing them all around his bed. In the middle of the night, his wife woke up with the feeling that there was somebody else in the room, and saw a faint glow of light at the foot of their bed. The next day, their neighbour came to see them. She told them that she had "visited" their bedroom last night and found that the bed was surrounded by triangles of fire. Lethbridge lost his scepticism instantly, and dedicated the rest of his life to investigating the paranormal.

Lethbridge's studies led him to believe that psychometry could be used in archaeology, that all things have a store of psychic energy within them which tells us of those who have previously owned or touched them. He also asserted that a pendulum can tell whether a skull belonged to a male or a female – if the pendulum swung back and forth, it was male; if it swung round in a circle, it was female. He also believed that psychometrists were in fact using telepathy, picking up information using objects as conduits to connect to the minds of others.

A very famous sceptic, though more famous for being the author of *Jurassic Park* among other novels, is Michael Crichton. In his autobiography, *Travels*, Crichton detailed an experiment that he performed in an effort to disprove psychic ability. He deliberately searched for psychics and withheld information from them. He did not tell them who he was, where he was from or what the purpose of his visit was, and when speaking to them, tried to maintain a non-committal body language. With one psychic, this proved fairly easy to do, as she was virtually blind and hard of hearing. When Crichton visited her, she suddenly said to him, "What on earth do you do for a living? Don't tell me, don't tell me. It's just that I can't put it together . . ." She then went on to describe that she had "seen" him working in what looked like a laundry room with large white baskets with black snakes coiling in them. She could see pictures running back-wards and forwards, and saw people wearing top hats and old-style fashion. She got all of this from touching Crichton. Crichton was amazed. Just before his visit to the psychic, he had been in the cutting room editing *The Great Train Robbery* which he was directing at the time. The film was set at the turn of the century with actors wearing top hats. In the editing room the film ran backwards and forwards through machinery, and fell into white baskets beneath the machinery. It could metaphorically have been described as coiled snakes.

The most amazing investigations into psychometry, however, have been conducted neither by sceptics nor scientists. In fact, these investigations have utilized the powers of psychometrists to amazing effect in investigations of an entirely different sort. The police have used the amazing abilities of psychometrists to catch elusive criminals, with some stunning successes, the most celebrated of which have centred around the Dutch psychic, Peter Hurkos.

Hurkos's career as a psychic began in 1941 following an accident on a building site. Hurkos fell four storeys, fracturing his skull, and was diagnosed as having concussion and possible brain damage. When he emerged from his coma four days later, he made two revelations. The first was to his doctor, whom he told, "Don't go! Something terrible will happen!" The doctor had been planning a trip overseas, and was not going to cancel because of the rantings of a patient. He was killed while on this holiday. His other revelation concerned his wife and son. Hurkos claimed that he heard his wife's voice in a dream. He awoke, screaming, "Bea [his wife's name], what are you doing here? Where's Benny? The whole room is burning with Benny." Just five days after this premonition, Hurkos's son Benny was trapped in a fire and rescued just in time. Both of these accounts are hearsay, and many sceptics believe that Hurkos in fact made them up to further his career as a theatrical psychic. He was a renowned self-publicist who became known throughout Europe as the man with "radar eyes", so you can see their point. Hurkos did, however, in the eyes of many, prove his psychic abilities through his collaborations with the police.

Hurkos's fame on the stage as a psychic brought him to the attention of the police in the Limburg province of Holland. A coal miner had been shot dead, and the authorities had no idea who had committed the crime, so they enlisted the help of Hurkos. Hurkos held the coat of the victim, and told the police that the murderer was Bernard van Tossing, the victim's stepfather. He also told the police that the murder weapon had been hidden on the roof of the victim's house. The gun was found on the roof, just as Hurkos had predicted it would be, and it was covered in van Tossing's fingerprints, securing his conviction for the murder of his stepson.

In 1948, Hurkos moved to America, and became as famous there as he had been throughout Europe. In due course he came to the attention of Charles Lipes, who was the chief of the homicide division in Miami. Lipes approached Hurkos to see if he could help in a murder enquiry. Hurkos was given a photograph of the murder victim, and also sat in a taxi that had been owned by the victim. He told Miami police that the murderer was known to his friends as "Smitty" and that he came from Detroit. He also stated that the murderer had killed someone else, in the Key West area. The police knew of the other murder, which had not been made public, but had never thought that the two incidents were connected. Forensic tests soon showed that the same gun had killed both victims. A month later, one Charles Smith, known to his friends as "Smitty", was tried and convicted of both murders.

The greatest test of Hurkos's psychometric abilities was made during the 1960s, during an investigation that had police utterly at a loss. A serial killer was on the loose in Boston, known as the "Boston Strangler", and the police had no idea who the evil killer could be. In 1964, Hurkos was secretly drafted into the investigation – secretly at Hurkos's own request, because he did not want to be hounded by the press.

Hurkos was picked up at the airport by Assistant Attorney-General John Bottomly and Detective Sergeant Leo Martin. When they stopped for coffee en route, Hurkos asked the Detective Sergeant who Katherine was. Martin explained that Katherine was his mother's name, and Hurkos replied, "You tell her, take doctor's advice. I am worried about her legs. Very bad varicose veins – she should do what family says." Martin and his family had been trying for a long time to get his mother to go to the hospital about her legs. Hurkos went on, describing how Martin's mother had just bought new glasses, and how she was currently suffering from chronic back pains. Bottomly informed Hurkos that he would be working alongside Julian Soshnick, and offered to describe him so that Hurkos would know him when they met. He didn't need to – Hurkos described Soshnick to Bottomly in meticulous detail, even down to his obsession with his own hair. The sceptics among us may question the validity of this – Hurkos knew that he was being called to work on the Boston Strangler case, and could easily have done research into the people he would be working with. Not so with Soshnick, who was not even on Bottomly's staff and had not yet started working on the case. He was chosen while Hurkos was on the plane and on the way to Boston.

Hurkos was given over 300 photographs from the scenes of the Boston Strangler's crimes, and on his very first session touching the photographs, he pulled one out and told the police, "This phoney baloney. This not belong." Soshnick had planted the photograph, which had been taken from a previously solved strangling case, to test the mettle of the psychic, and the psychic had come up to scratch. For the next six days, working for eighteen hours a day, Hurkos studied the photographs and other evidence provided by the police. He did not look at the photographs, merely touched the backs of them, and described in detail the events which happened at the scenes as if he were there, including many things which had been kept secret from the public. He described in detail the appearance of the Strangler himself: he was around 5 feet 7 inches (1.7 m), had a scar on his left arm from an accident at work, had a "spitzy" nose and some damage to his thumb. He also said that the Strangler slept on a bed with no mattress, only springs, and that he took showers with his clothes on.

A real breakthrough came when the police handed Hurkos a letter written to the Boston School of Nursing by a man who wished to interview a nurse for a magazine article and possible marriage. Hurkos held the letter and, without reading it, declared that the writer of the letter was the killer, a homosexual misogynist aged fifty-two who spoke with a French accent. Hurkos's descriptions led to the arrest of a man whom the police referred to as Thomas P. O'Brien (his true identity was withheld), whose identity and background matched Hurkos's descriptions very closely. The police, however, did not have sufficient evidence to bring the case to trial, and opted to have "O'Brien" temporarily committed to a mental institution for observation. "O'Brien" voluntarily committed himself indefinitely which made it legally impossible for him to be tried for murder.

The police, however, began to suspect a different man, who also fitted many of Hurkos's descriptions. The man in question was Albert DeSalvo, who had already been arrested for a series of rapes, and committed to the same mental institution as "O'Brien" for treatment for schizophrenia. While in the institution, DeSalvo boasted about the eleven murders he had committed, the murders in question being those of the Boston Strangler. He also provided evidence which had not been made available to the public in his confessions to the police. Moreoever,

DeSalvo had a "spitzy" nose and a scar on his left arm which he had acquired from an injury at work. Ironically, he never stood trial, for exactly the same reasons as "O'Brien", but he has entered the history books as being the Boston Strangler. DeSalvo is now dead, and has taken the mystery with him to his grave. The police accepted his confession without hesitation and closed the case, mainly due to his knowledge of facts which had not been made public. But in doing so the police ignored the protestations of Hurkos, who always believed that DeSalvo was not the Boston Strangler. It is possible that DeSalvo was an unfortunate combination – an unbalanced person who would confess to crimes he had not committed, and someone who himself had a psychic ability which informed him of the evidence he needed to make his confession believable. We will never know the truth, only that Hurkos, who had been right on so many occasions throughout the investigation, was convinced that the police had a confession from the wrong man.

Of course, it is also possible that Hurkos did in fact get it wrong. Psychometrists describe the process of psychometry as receiving and interpreting impressions. Sometimes they will interpret the impressions erroneously; every psychometrist does this, even the most famous and respected, but those who most often come to the fore have a higher number of hits than misses.

Another successful psychometrist, and one who also aided the police, is Gerard Croiset, who, like Hurkos, hailed from Holland. Croiset first discovered his ability as a child when he held a ruler owned by a local watchmaker, and saw scenes from the watchmaker's life in his head. During the 1940s, Croiset came under the wing of parapsychologist Professor Willem Tenhaeff, who put Croiset through a series of psychiatric and psychic tests at the University of Utrecht. Tenhaeff had tested dozens of psychics over a twenty-year period, but he claimed that Croiset was his most gifted subject. During the time that Croiset spent with Tenhaeff, his fame steadily grew and, over the years, he was consulted by police forces from Europe, America and China to help them solve cases that had them baffled.

As a psychometrist, Croiset is intriguing. The field of psychometry deals with psychics who can pick up impressions simply by touching them, yet Croiset was able to sense things over the telephone, without even touching the objects in question. A handful of other psychometrists also claim to have this ability, and they regard the phenomenon as being able to "touch" the sounds as they come out of the receiver. The following case clearly reveals how this technique works.

A four-year-old girl disappeared on 22 February 1961 in New York. She was still missing on 25 February when an official of the Dutch airline KLM located Croiset and offered to fly him to New York to help solve the case. Croiset declared that he had never been to New York, and that all the new impressions he might pick up in the big city would cloud his ability to help in the case. He asked instead to be sent photographs of the child, a map of New York and an item of her clothing. However, before he hung up the telephone, Croiset started to talk to the official about the case, and to sense what had happened. He then told the official that the girl was dead, and he described in fairly vague terms where her body was to be found: in a tall building with billboards on its roof, near an elevated railroad and a river. He also described her killer as a small man aged about fifty-four or fifty-five, who wore grey. The next day, the materials Croiset had asked for were flown in from New York, and he psychometrized them. He gleaned further clues from this evidence: he got a very strong emotion about the second floor of the building, and now decided that the murderer was a little older, between fifty-four and fifty-eight, with a "small, sharp, tawny face".

About six hours later, as part of a routine search unconnected with the missing girl, New York police broke into a second-storey room in a four-storey block, and found the girl's body. The building was located near an elevated railroad and the Hudson river. The landlord of the building identified the man who rented the room, who was later arrested and convicted of the girl's murder. He was a small man in his fifties, with a sharp, pointed nose, and was dressed predominantly in grey.

Perhaps the most famous British case to include evidence from psychics was the case of the Yorkshire Ripper, who murdered thirteen women over a period of five years beginning in 1975. He would mutilate two or three women over two or three days, then disappear for months before resuming his activities once more. Many psychics offered their impressions to newspapers and the police, including Doris Stokes, an internationally famous clairaudient. Doris alleged that the killer was called Ronnie or Johnny, was about 5 feet 8 inches tall (1.72 m), and lived in Tyneside. Stokes, along with many other psychics, was way off the mark.

Nella Jones, however, pretty much hit the bull's-eye. Sixteen months before the killer was captured, Nella gave a description of the killer to a reporter who worked for a local newspaper, the *Yorkshire Post*. She said that the Ripper's name was Peter, and he was a truck driver who worked for a company beginning with the letter "C", which she had "seen" on the side of his truck; she said that he lived at number six on a street in Bradford, a house which was raised above the street and had steps up to the front door. When the killer was tracked down by the police in January 1980, he turned out to be Peter Sutcliffe of 6 Garden Lane, Bradford. His house matched the description given by Nella Jones. He had also been working as a truck driver for a company called Clark Transport, and the name appeared on all their vehicles. Sutcliffe was not, however, as Nella had also predicted, a transvestite.

Psychometrists therefore encounter a varying mixture of success and failure in their predictions. The mixed results and lack of admissible evidence that psychometrists provide limit their use in police investigations, but the cases shown above prove that they can help alongside more usual police routines. The next time a case has a police force utterly at a loss, they will no doubt call in the inexplicable services of a psychic.

The Mind and Beyond
••••••••••••••••••••••••••••••••••••

The brain, the mind and the psychic

The human brain is a complex mass of nerve cells called neurons, and supporting cells known as neuroglia. Most of these trillions of cells are located within the cerebral cortex – the layer of grey matter that lies over the rest of the brain, and is believed to be the centre of consciousness and thought. Cells on the surface of the cerebral cortex process information received from the outside world, from our eyes, ears, nose, mouth and touch, and the data is then passed on to the interior of the cerebral cortex. Once there, the information is combined with data from memory and other areas of the brain to create the feelings, thoughts, images and ideas that make up an individual.

Scientists now know that the information dealt with by the brain is processed by the neurons through electrical impulses. But how these impulses become our thoughts and feelings still remains a mystery. The most recent research shows that we do not have one brain, but three, each of which differs from the other two in structure and function, yet they are all interrelated. Through the process of evolution, the three masses of neurons have become superimposed upon each other.

The first and most ancient of these brain areas has

been named the "R-complex" or reptilian brain, and is believed to contain our survival instincts such as hunting, fighting and mating. Surrounding the R-complex is the limbic system, which links humans to other mammals, and is believed to regulate emotion, memory and certain aspects of movement. The cerebral cortex makes up the third area of the brain. It is believed to be the newest addition to the human brain, evolving only over the last two million years or so, and is much more developed in humans than in any other animal. The cerebral cortex is what separates humankind from other animals, and controls our ability to reason, think abstractly, form symbols and create culture and language.

The discovery that the human brain has different regions responsible for different processes has led to several explanations for the difference between the conscious and the unconscious mind. One theory was put forward by the British psychologist Stan Gooch. Gooch argued that a human is in fact a dual being, consisting of a rational "ego" – the part of the being that is considered the real self – and a darker, more intuitive "self". Gooch believes that the ego is located in the cerebral cortex, the most recent addition to the brain, and that the self inhabits a part of the more ancient limbic area of the brain, which he termed the cerebellum. The cerebellum controls muscular activity and, according to Gooch, is also the seat of the unconscious. It is from the cerebellum that the brain creates dreams.

Gooch also believes that the cerebellum is responsible for paranormal experiences. In his book, *The Paranormal*, he describes how he had a mediumistic trance when he went to a séance with a friend:

"Suddenly it seemed to me that a great wind was rushing through the room. In my ears was the deafening sound of roaring waters. As I felt myself swept away I became unconscious."

When Gooch woke up, he was told by others present at the séance that several spirits had spoken through him. He felt as though he had been possessed, and described the sensation as though the spirits had slipped on his body much as he would slip on a suit. In Gooch's opinion, the source of such mystical, paranormal experiences lies deep within the ancient parts of the brain.

Other researchers, however, argue that paranormal events are controlled by parts of the brain much closer to the surface – in the right hemisphere of the cerebral cortex. We now know that the two halves of the cerebral cortex, though they are exact mirror images of each other, serve completely different functions. The left hemisphere controls the right side of the body, and is responsible for verbal reasoning, deciphering abstract symbols, logical thinking and working with numbers. The right hemisphere controls the left side of the body, and controls non-verbal, intuitive thought. The right hemisphere is thought by most to be the source of creativity and a certain cosmic wisdom responsible for such powers as ESP.

This theory gained much weight in the 1940s, with the development of a radical surgical technique for severe epilepsy. The procedure involved, effectively, splitting the brain in two, thereby making it impossible for the left and right hemispheres to communicate with each other. Prior to this invention, many patients who had suffered from epilepsy had died from extensive brain damage caused when a seizure crossed from one brain hemisphere to the other. Surgeons found that by cutting the brain, they could limit the damage to only one side of the brain. The technique at first seemed to be extremely successful, not only reducing the damaging effects of an epileptic fit, but making no obvious change in the patient's personality or in their intellectual abilities. But subtle changes had indeed taken effect, and these only became fully apparent after twenty years, when scientists made extensive tests on split-brain patients.

The scientists found that the way in which the brain coped with different messages had changed quite dramatically. In one case, a patient who had undergone a split-brain operation was studied by Roger Sperry and Michael Gazzaniga of the California Institute of Technology. The two hemispheres of her brain were found to be capable of working simultaneously on different tasks. The patient was placed before a split-screen monitor, and the doctors flashed the word *clap* to her right hemisphere, and the word *laugh* to the left. She immediately laughed and clapped, but when asked, she replied that she had only seen the word laugh on the screen. Her right hemisphere could not verbalize the command it had seen, but could carry it out, even at the same time that the left brain was executing the order to clap.

This, and other results, led to speculation that within every individual there are two separate selves, one personality living within the left hemisphere of the brain, the other on the right. Gazzaniga concluded that each hemisphere has its own memories and emotions. Problems can occur when the two hemispheres have different values. For example, when Gazzaniga asked the right hemisphere of a patient what he wanted to be, he replied that he wished to be a racing driver. When Gazzaniga asked the left, the patient responded that he wanted to be a draughtsman.

Damage to the brain does not always have a negative effect, however. Occasionally, a change will occur in the brain that enhances the five senses, or even unleashes what many believe to be the sixth. Many scientists now believe that many phenomena associated with the sixth sense, such as telepathy, clairvoyance and psychometry, are really the result of one or more of the ordinary five senses becoming hyperactive in a supernormal way.

One such phenomenon is synesthesia, a very rare condition whereby the five senses are intermingled in such a way that a person can *see* sounds, *feel* colours and *taste* words. To someone who has the condition, the sound of a telephone ringing may look like a swirl of colours, or the word *computer* may taste like a hamburger. The most common form of the affliction is coloured hearing, where a person can see sounds.

Neurologist Richard Cytowic performed extensive tests on synesthetic people. He discovered that when they were experiencing the phenomenon, the blood flow through their brains altered. Normally, blood flow increases in the cerebral cortex during stimulation of the five senses, but Cytowic found that during synesthesic behaviour, the blood flow decreased in the cerebral cortex, and increased in the more ancient limbic system. According to Cytowic, "The brain's higher information processing turns off during coloured hearing. An older, more fundamental way of viewing the world . . . takes over." In other words, these rare individuals were shutting off the modern part of their brains, and a part that has lain dormant for millions of years had been accessed. Many scientists now believe that this could, to a greater or lesser extent, explain the psychic abilities of certain individuals. It is possible that we all have extraordinary abilities, but that our brain no longer accesses these areas due to our evolutionary growth. The rational side of the brain has become all-powerful, cutting off our psychic area.

Another aspect of the synesthesia condition is known as skin vision, or eyeless sight. Now classified as a neurological disorder, it had for centuries been thought of as a psychic power, and still is today. This strange phenomenon was first investigated in Russia, when a young Russian woman named Rosa Kuleshova confounded scientists at the Biophysics Institute of the Soviet Academy of Sciences. She was able to read printed words and distinguish colours using only her fingers, even while blindfolded. The Russian scientists devoted many hours of research into the phenomenon and eventually managed to train one in six of their subjects to differentiate between colours simply by touch. Those who were successful reported that yellow felt slippery, orange was rough and that each colour radiated its texture to a certain height, enabling many to tell which colour it was simply by passing their hand over it, actually touching it wasn't necessary.

All manner of brain disorders manifest in the individual exceptional abilities. People with "savant syndrome" can display quite extraordinary gifts, such as amazing feats of memory. The memory of savants, however, is a seemingly unconscious form of memory. It shows absolutely no sign of self-reflection, no cognitive awareness and no emotional involvement. What tends to be the case is that these exceptional people can remember any length of numbers or sequences, but cannot even remember their own name or where they live. The disorder can manifest itself in other ways also.

Alonzo Clemens suffered an injury to his brain when he was three and, as a result, in adult life he had an IQ of just forty, could barely count to ten, and had the vocabulary of a two-year-old child. Yet his ability as an artist has flowered, and he can mould a lump of clay with incredible detail into any animal, showing every muscle and sinew. His art sells around the world for staggering sums, and is considered by connoisseurs to be among the best. Leslie Lemke, another savant, is blind, mentally retarded and suffers from cerebral palsy. He does, however, have fantastic musical talents. He can play a piece of music perfectly after hearing it only once, whether classical or rock, and after listening to a forty-five-minute tape just once, he can play it directly on the piano. As he plays, he also sings the opera's libretto in the language in which it was sung on the tape.

Artistic and musical genius are relatively common among savants. Many of them also show signs of extra-sensory perception, as seen in a study published by Bernard Rimland, a psychologist in San Diego. The parents of many young savants in the study noticed their children's uncanny abilities, such as opening the door for them when they returned home, knowing that they were there, hearing conversations that were out of earshot and picking up on thoughts which were not spoken. A leading neurologist, Darold Treffert, believes that these psychic abilities are caused by damage to the left hemisphere of the brain, usually incurred prior to birth. The right hemisphere of the brain then compensates for the damage to the left, and becomes overdeveloped, causing an imbalance of the brain. The right-brain skills therefore become super-developed, enabling amazing feats which have previously been thought of as psychic abilities or paranormal phenomena.

Treffert strongly believes that the significance of such syndromes as savant syndrome and autism "lies in our inability to explain it. The savants stand as a clear reminder of our ignorance about ourselves, especially about how our brains function. For no model of brain function, particularly memory, will be complete until it can include and account for this remarkable condition." Many other scientists agree, and see the study of such disorders as the most likely way to explore the links between the human brain, the mind and psychic ability. Perhaps it is the science of neurology that will finally unlock the mysteries of the psychics?

Me, myself and I

Unusual mental states can often lead to types of behaviour often regarded as paranormal. Psychic ability is very often found among sufferers of multiple personality disorder, a relatively new label given to an age-old affliction. In different cultures or ages, the symptoms now associated with multiple personality disorder were regarded as evidence of divine inspiration, demonic possession or mediumistic trance.

In the modern world, most scientists who study such mental disorders point to psychological or physiological deficiencies as the cause of the problems. There are many, however, who suggest that such disorders as multiple personalities, schizophrenia and even creative geniuses, may be tapping into a collective unconscious, a higher reality where all objects and events are linked to others. In fact, some brave psychologists have even stated the view that mental illness is not so much a failure to cope with reality, as a successful journey into another, hidden realm.

Multiple personality disorder has been repeatedly linked to paranormal phenomena. Many researchers believe that not all the personalities manifested by a sufferer are created by the sufferer. Some, it is suggested, may be spirits from another realm, or possibly parts of previous lives reasserting themselves in their new incarnation. In the 1980s, an American psychiatrist, Ralph Allison, came up with the term "Inner Self Helper" to describe a special personality that helps the patient to heal themselves. Personalities of this type often claim to be channellers for divine love and healing power, and Allison put forward the idea that they may in fact enter the patient from an outside power:

> "The discovery of an entity who doesn't serve any recognizable purpose presents a diagnostic problem. Such entities often refer to themselves as spirits. Over the years I've encountered too many such cases to dismiss the possibility of spirit possession completely."

One such Inner Self Helper became apparent in the famous case of Katherine Castle, who began treatment for her multiple personality disorder in the 1980s. Her therapy revealed that her core self had begun to shatter during childhood. Katherine had many personalities, among them a guardian angel called Michael, who was described by her other personalities as a kindly man in a dark hat and coat. Michael first manifested himself on the day that a friend of Katherine's family died before her eyes in a stock-car racing crash.

Many years after his first appearance, one of Katherine's personalities called "Me-Liz" saw Michael at the beach. This time, he was not alone.

"Behind and above him, hanging in the air like three flashing, ghostly cymbals, were the beings."

According to the Me-Liz personality, Michael had told Katherine that these beings would appear, and that they would "signify a great new unfolding in her life. Something grand and wonderful was preparing to take place". As Katherine's therapy progressed, Michael and these beings of light helped in the healing process. These beings apparently convinced Katherine's multiple personalities to fuse back into one whole. The process came to a climax in what Katherine described as an intense experience of bright lights and a whirling sensation supervised by Michael. At the end of this experience, Katherine emerged as just the one personality – herself.

Different people in Katherine's life have different views on just what Michael was. Her psychiatrist believes that Michael was a part of Katherine's unconscious brain helping to repair the trauma of her life. Her church minister fully believes that Michael was a separate being altogether. When Katherine's healing process was over, he wrote:

> *"I considered Michael to be an angel. I believe in angels. I know God speaks, and he speaks to people in different ways."*

Another analyst, Joseph Pearce, compares the Inner Self Helper to the Buddhist concept of the *tulpa*. The tulpa is a phantasmic spirit-self that passes from one generation to the next, and is usually hidden from the conscious self. This tulpa can emerge to act as a healer, and it is believed that the Tibetan monks can make it appear at will. Whatever the reason for the Inner Self Helper, be it a spirit, a psychic healing power or a defence mechanism generated by the brain, it certainly worked in Katherine's case. But it is true that sufferers of multiple personality disorder seem exceptionally open to paranormal events of many kinds.

Chris Sizemore is one of the most famous sufferers of multiple personality disorder, and has become the subject of several books, among them *The Three Faces of Eve*, *I'm Eve* and *A Mind of my Own*. While suffering from her disorder, she became prone to precognitive visions. On one occasion, she convinced her husband to stay at home because she feared that if he went to work, he would be electrocuted. A co-worker who took over her husband's shift because of his absence was electrocuted on the job that very day.

There are also reports of people with multiple personalities apparently able to absorb energy.

Psychiatrist Ralph Allison has noted that he felt physically sapped of energy while in the presence of a patient with multiple personality disorder. Even more astonishingly, a nineteenth-century multiple personality disorder sufferer called Mollie Fancher was said to kill small animals by draining their life force. A psychic researcher called Scott Rogo interviewed Ralph Allison about this energy-sapping phenomenon. When asked how many of his patients afflicted with multiple personality disorder had paranormal abilities, Allison replied:

"Every one of them. It may be the primary personality that has some ability to tell what's coming up in the future for her kids, or accidents they're going to get into. That happens quite frequently. If the patient has a lot of personalities, there will be one who is very psychic, and the others will have average ability or no abilities."

Research into multiple personalities, therefore, might explain some paranormal claims, and it may also provide insight into the workings of the mind. The disorder is certainly a clear indication that the conscious mind is not always aware of what is happening in other parts of the brain. Some evidence from abnormally functioning brains shows that the mind is capable of working in quite exceptional ways when it seeks to ignore the rules. There is no reason to believe that "normal" people can't also access these talents, if only they knew *how* to access them. Perhaps savants, and people with multiple personalities, have recovered parts of the brain that the rest of us have forgotten through the process of evolution?

Journeying beyond the mind

Every culture in history has sought to extend the perceptions of the mind beyond what is deemed to be normal. Buddhists strive to achieve this higher state of consciousness through a lifetime of discipline and meditation, as do the Indian fakirs. In the Western world, achieving this transcendent journey has tended to be less mystical and more induced by drugs.

In the period following World War II, researchers in the West began to experiment with such hallucinogenic drugs as lysergic acid diethylamide (LSD). They discovered that tiny doses of these drugs were capable of producing powerful hallucinations. During the early period of research into the drugs, little was known about the negative effects, and the funding in America came mainly from government institutions. The CIA, for example, believed that the drugs could be used as weapons to break down the resolve of enemy spies. Research results soon indicated that LSD could even replicate the symptoms of psychosis, but the research continued unabated until the mid-1960s, when the government classed the drugs as illegal.

One of the "pioneers" of LSD research was a maverick psychologist called Timothy Leary. Leary became interested in mind-altering substances after a "trip" he experienced in 1960 on "magic mushrooms". The episode seemed to change his life radically:

"I laughed at my own everyday pomposity, the narrow arrogance of scholars, the impudence of

the rational, the smug naivete of words in contrast to the raw rich ever-changing panoramas that flooded my brain. I gave way to delight, as mystics have for centuries when they peeked through the curtains and discovered that this world – so manifestly real – was actually a tiny stage set constructed by the mind. There was a sea of possibilities out there, other realities, an infinite array of programs for other futures."

Leary's journey beyond the normal limits of his mind lasted for about four hours. When he returned to normal, he felt that he had done more to investigate the mysteries of the mind in those four hours than he had in fifteen years as a psychologist. He became convinced that the modern brain is only partially used, and that it was capable of a far greater intelligence and a higher state of consciousness. Leary felt that extraordinary powers were waiting to be unleashed, and that psychedelic drugs were the key to open the door of the mind.

Leary established a research programme at his university to explore the issue further. In tests on over 200 subjects, he found that 85 per cent of them said that the experience was the most educational of their lives, but there was no way of showing that the subjects' lives had been altered in any way. Leary soon found a way to test that hypothesis.

He was invited by a nearby state prison to test the effects of the drugs on volunteer inmates. Leary's work with them proved relatively successful. The convicts experienced the same mind-opening phenomena that had sparked Leary's interest into hallucinogenic drugs in the first place. In the second year of the programme, Leary's subjects appeared to benefit quite dramatically from their experiences. They suddenly perceived new possibilities for life outside prison, and within a year of release, only about 10 per cent of those on parole were back in jail. This compared with the 70 per cent return rate for untreated prisoners.

Such research led Leary to believe that psychedelic drugs could play a huge role in treating the ills of society. He published a manual for his mystical ministrations entitled *The Psychedelic Journey*, in which he predicted that his scientific drug programme could work for the benefit of society by helping people to explore the hidden realms of the mind. Soon after the publication of his book, however, it became apparent to Leary that Western society did not view drug-induced altered states of consciousness in quite the same light as he did. By 1966, stringent new laws were introduced which brought psychedelic research pretty much to a halt. Scientists in the field were asked to return their supplies of drugs to the manufacturers, and Leary became an outsider within the scientific community. Eventually, he served a prison term for his beliefs in the drug culture. The US government's dabbling into drug culture had, however, sparked off a movement which refused to go away. A generation of people had experienced the higher state of consciousness associated with LSD, and despite the government's efforts, they continued to take it.

Increasingly strenuous drug laws and disillusionment with the negative effects of the chemicals led people to seek different ways of expanding their minds. It soon became a fad to turn to Eastern mysticism to achieve a heightened sense of consciousness through meditation, which many found produced purer and longer lasting "highs" than those achieved through drugs. Meditation is also, of course, free of the negative side effects of drugs, such as nausea.

The most famous proponent of such mind expanding techniques was Maharishi Mahesh Yogi, who taught a form of meditation called Transcendental Meditation. He achieved great fame when The Beatles embraced his philosophies for a few months in 1967. Transcendental meditation requires devotees to meditate twice daily, repeating an individually assigned mantra. It claims to have produced such psychic powers as levitation and invulnerability (safety from all assault, both physical and spiritual). However, the Maharishi's teachings were less concerned with such powers than with a greater philosophy. His meditative techniques were designed to "turn the attention inward, putting the conscious mind in contact with the creative intelligence that gives rise to every thought". He claimed that his techniques could create a "wave of coherence and harmony" that would decisively cure the world's problems and bring about "heaven on Earth for all mankind on a permanent basis".

Interest in the Maharishi's teachings has declined considerably over the last thirty years. Despite many devotees meditating furiously, many of his claims remain unfulfilled. At one stage, he claimed to have discovered the secret of age reversal, though his own ageing process seems to be going along quite nicely. Tens of thousands of devotees took his course in levitation, yet none can lift themselves off the ground without physical force. But interest in a higher state of consciousness persists, because it is known that it exists, and that it can unleash a number of psychic powers. Whether it can be brought about by drugs or meditation is another unanswered question. There is some agreement, however, that accessing a higher state of consciousness and bestowing upon oneself paranormal abilities is possible by tapping into parts of the brain which have lain dormant for millions of years. Quite how these areas can be awoken is as yet unknown.

The Psychics

••••••••••••••••••••••••••••••••••

Throughout history, certain individuals have been
marked out, or have marked themselves out, as
having abilities which the rest of us do not have. From
the Oracle at Delphi to Uri Geller, Nostradamus to
Doris Stokes, these individuals have held their
contemporaries in thrall at the amazing powers of
their minds. In this chapter, we shall look at just six of
these amazing individuals: Nostradamus, Eileen
Garrett, Sai Baba, Doris Stokes, Uri Geller and Edgar
Cayce.

Nostradamus

Michel de Nostredame was born on 14 December
1503 in Provence, France. His great intellect became
apparent while he was still very young, as did his
interest in astronomy. He would talk with his fellow
students about his belief in the Copernican theory
that the Earth revolved around the sun, a belief he
upheld more than one hundred years before Galileo
was prosecuted for espousing the same views.
Nostradamus trained as a doctor, and soon became
known for his tireless work helping plague victims in
France. Most of Nostradamus's fellow physicians fled

Nostradamus – The greatest prophet that ever lived?

from areas infested with the plague, inadvertently helping its spread. Nostradamus stayed put, and was alone throughout many an epidemic, working among the sick, curing many, and insisting on fresh air and unpolluted water when the thinking of the time was to drain blood from the victims.

Nostradamus started work on *The Centuries* in 1554, a book of prophecies that were to contain predictions from his time to the end of the world. The books were called *The Centuries*, not because they were in some chronological order, but because each book contained one hundred verses. The verses were written in an obscure style, in a mixture of languages including French, Provençal, Italian, Greek and Latin. Nostradamus explained that the reason that the prophecies were so obscure was to avoid prosecution as a magician and heretic by religious authorities.

Nostradamus is now probably the only author who could claim that his work has never been out of print for over four hundred years, apart from the Bible. On average, thirty books about his prophecies have been published every century since his death in 1566. Many different interpretations have been offered of *The Centuries*, as might be expected of such a cryptic collection of verses, and some of the results have been startling. If his prophetic powers are to be believed, and the interpretations of them are accurate, then Nostradamus has predicted some of the most crucial events in world history. Many interpreters of his works believe that Nostradamus predicted the rise and fall of Napoleon; the threat posed by Hitler; the tragedy surrounding the Kennedy family; the bombing of Hiroshima; a third world war; and the end of the world.

In 1939, shortly after the German invasion of Poland, Frau Goebbels was lying in bed, reading a book which contained some predictions made four centuries earlier by Nostradamus. Her husband was Dr Goebbels, the chief of the Nazi Propaganda Ministry. Frau Goebbels woke her husband excitedly, and made him read two passages from the prophetic work. Goebbels was so impressed by the revelations that he arranged for them to be reprinted and dropped on enemy troops as a propaganda exercise. Naturally, he changed the wording quite radically, but the gist of the message was the same: Hitler was here, and Hitler was going to win.

The two verses are perhaps Nostradamus's most famous, for they come very close to naming Hitler, and described his destructive activities with some accuracy. According to the first one:

"Liberty shall not be recovered, a black, fierce, villainous, evil man shall occupy it, when the ties of his alliance are wrought. Venice shall be vexed by Hister."

The second of these verses was even more vivid:

"Beasts wild with hunger will cross the rivers, the greater part of the battlefield will be against Hister. He will drag the leader in a cage of iron, when the child of Germany observes no law."

Many people have tried to interpret these two verses in the light of Hitler's rise to power and the horrors which followed. The word "Hister" is obviously considered to be Nostradamus foreseeing

"Hitler". The cage of iron could well be a tank, although many believe this to be the blockades upon Britain during the early years of the war, when Britain alone stood against the evils of the Third Reich. Most of the rest is self-explanatory – the "child of Germany" certainly did not obey any international laws; Germany crossed many rivers; Venice, along with many other cities, was annexed by Germany.

"Hister" also appeared in several other verses, sometimes referred to directly by that name, often as the "child of Germany", or by other inference. Many translators of Nostradamus's work have pointed to two other verses, which have been interpreted as dealing with Hitler's disappearance at the end of the war. One suggests that he was buried alive in his bunker, the other that he disappeared. The first one reads as follows:

> *"The fortress of the besieged shut up by gunpowder sunk into its depths; the traitor will be entombed alive, never did so pitiful a schism happen to the sextons."*

This has often been interpreted as referring to Hitler and the few of his followers who remained in the fortified bunker to be shelled by the Allies. The other verse which many believe refers to Hitler's disappearance reads as follows:

> *"Near the Rhine from the Norican mountains will be born a great man of the people, come too late. He will defend Poland and Hungary and they will never know what became of him."*

Hitler was born in Noricum (Austria), and he was the son of simple parents. Perhaps he "came too late" in Nostradamus's point of view, because his type of empire was outdated. Hitler described his attacks on Poland and Hungary as "saving" them from the Allies. The last line is the most talked about. The bodies found in the bunker were never identified as being those of Hitler and Eva Braun – is it possible that they escaped? As Hitler's body was never recovered, this is a debate (though a fairly pointless one) which still rages today.

Another recurring theme in *The Centuries* is "the three brothers". Most modern interpretations agree that these three brothers are in fact the Kennedy brothers: John, Robert and Edward. If viewed in this light, then it would appear that Nostradamus foresaw the deaths of the three brothers, including a very interesting revelation on John F. Kennedy's assassination. The most startling of the revelations reads as follows:

> *"The great man will be struck down in the day by a thunderbolt. An evil deed, foretold by the bearer of a petition. According to the prediction another falls at night time. Conflict at Reims, London and pestilence in Tuscany."*

The great man in question is interpreted as being John Kennedy, who was shot dead in broad daylight, supposedly by the evil deed committed by Lee Harvey Oswald. The event had been foretold by Jeane Dixon, the "Washington Seer", who had tried unsuccessfully to warn the president of his forthcoming death. Dixon also predicted the death of Robert Kennedy, who was assassinated during the early hours of the morning while celebrating his victory in the presidential primary elections. The conflict at Reims and London most likely refers to the international repercussions following these assassinations, including student riots in Britain and France immediately afterwards. The pestilence in Tuscany could well refer to a flood which occurred in Florence around the time.

If John Kennedy is, as is thought, referred to throughout *The Centuries* as "the great man", then another of Nostradamus's prophecies which also refers to his assassination is one which has caused, perhaps, the greatest controversy. Lee Harvey Oswald has been written into the history books as his assassin, but there has been much debate over this fact ever since that fateful day. Many think that Kennedy was assassinated as part of a CIA conspiracy, and we all know the story surrounding the number of gunshots, and the likelihood that Oswald did not fire them all. This verse, if taken to refer to the assassination of John F. Kennedy, seems to espouse Oswald's innocence:

> *"The ancient work will be accomplished, and from the roof evil ruin will fall on to the great man. Being dead, they will accuse an innocent of the deed, the guilty one hidden in the misty woods."*

It is now widely believed that JFK was killed by gunshots fired from more than one location. One was the book depository roof, from where Lee Harvey Oswald was allegedly seen leaving. The other was a grassy knoll by the side of the highway. Some forensic scientists concluded that it was from here that the fatal shot to Kennedy's head was fired – was the real killer "hidden in the misty woods"? As for Oswald, he was never officially found guilty – he was himself shot by Jack Ruby prior to his trial.

The "great man" crops up many times in *The Centuries* often, as above, referring to his all-too-sudden and untimely demise. The verse below has been interpreted as once again referring to this, but also to the Cuban missile crisis of 1962:

> *"Before the battle the great man will fall, the great one to death, death too sudden and lamented. Born imperfect, it will go the greater part of the way; near the river of blood the ground is stained."*

John Kennedy's death was indeed very sudden and lamented the world over. The interesting part of this verse is "it will go the greater part of the way", which many believe refers to the Cuban missile crisis, when Kennedy stood up against Mr Khrushchev's attempt to set up Soviet missile bases in Cuba. The Russian fleet did, after all, get the greater part of the way from Russia, and the world braced itself for a nuclear holocaust. Eventually, Khrushchev did back down, and it was shortly after this that Kennedy was assassinated.

Robert Kennedy took over as the hopeful presidential candidate in the Kennedy dynasty when his brother was assassinated. Nostradamus, again according to many interpretations, also predicted that he would be assassinated shortly after his brother:

> *"The successor will avenge his handsome brother and occupy the realm under the shadow of vengeance, he, killed, the obstacle of the blame-*

> *worthy dead, his blood; for a long time Britain will hold with France."*

Nostradamus foresaw two brothers killed within a short period of time. Robert Kennedy was indeed assassinated shortly after his brother; his stand for president in the name of John ("under the shadow of vengeance") did him no good. The next in line in the dynasty is Edward Kennedy, who has made it to senator. What does Nostradamus see in the future for him?

> *"A great king captured by the hands of a young man, not far from Easter, confusion, a state of the knife. Everlasting captives, times when the lightning is on the top, when three brothers will be wounded and murdered."*

As mentioned before, the theme of the three brothers from America runs through Nostradamus's prophecies, and this verse indicates that all three brothers are murdered, and that one of the killings could happen around Easter, with perhaps a storm thrown in, the "lightning on top". Since John Kennedy died on 22 November 1963, and Robert Kennedy on 6 June 1968, perhaps Nostradamus is predicting here another death which will occur near Easter? Time will tell.

Believers in Nostradamus's prophecies will recently have been praying for their souls. As a prophet, he very rarely put a date on his predictions. Most famously, he mentioned the number 666 when predicting the Great Fire of London, which happened in 1666, but he also appears to have become very specific when talking of Armageddon, the battle which marks the end of the world:

> *"In the year 1999, and seven months, from the sky will come the great King of Terror. He will bring back to life the great king of the Mongols. Before and after War reigns happily."*

In this gloomy prediction, Nostradamus seems to foresee the end of the world around the time of the millennium, or to be specific, the seventh month of 1999, namely July. He also foresees war before and after this period. Yet Nostradamus's predictions continue for many years after the supposed end of the world, something which has baffled interpreters for centuries. If this verse is to be taken literally, then it is an abject failure. July 1999 came and went, but the world did not go with it. Nostradamus's predictions for the end of the world have also been synonymous with the appearance of Halley's comet, which first appeared this century in 1910. Many believed that the end of the world would happen when the comet next appeared – which it did, according to its seventy-six-year orbit, in 1986. Nothing happened. The comet is next due to appear in the year 2062 – perhaps *that* year will signal the end of the world.

The works of Nostradamus will, no doubt, keep people guessing for a long time to come. He managed to produce more prophecies than any other seer in history, and many people are convinced of the veracity of his visions of the future. I leave the discussion on Nostradamus with a comment from the famous debunker, James Randi:

"His reputation, however, is due to the ardent horde of his disciples who continue to this day to hyperbolize, bowdlerize, and invent in order to perpetuate his fame."

In other words, almost anything can be read into Nostradamus's prophecies to make them fit. Some may well be true but, for all we know, we could, over the years, have interpreted them all completely incorrectly, and Nostradamus could be laughing at us from his grave. I personally think that it is a waste of time trying to predict the future from an analysis of *The Centuries*. The prophecies which have "come to be" could not have been analysed until such time as the event they supposedly referred to had already happened. Nothing concrete can come of trying to interpret Nostradamus's revelations, as no one's prior interpretation will be taken seriously unless the event happens. One only has to look at the number of foolish people who were convinced that the world was going to end in July 1999.

Eileen Garrett

Eileen Garrett was born Eileen Jeanette Vancho in County Meath, Ireland. She grew up in the shadow of a mystical hill called Tara in a countryside where, she claims, "the 'little people' were universally accepted as an everyday part of normal existence". She claims that growing up in such a landscape is one of the main reasons for the manifestation of her psychic powers.

Both Garrett's parents committed suicide when she was only an infant, her first husband died in action during World War I, and only one of her four children survived into adulthood. This could go a long way to explain why Garrett refused to believe that death was the ultimate end to life, and why she was so ready to accept the ability to communicate with the spirit world.

Garrett left Ireland as a young woman, and lived in London and then the South of France before moving to New York and taking on American citizenship. She had a successful career in publishing, but soon realized that her real calling lay with the paranormal. In 1951, she founded the Parapsychology Foundation, whose aim it was to research into the paranormal. Through the organization she funded expeditions all over the world to explain psychic powers. Her enthusiasm for all things psychic and the occult was legendary – she studied voodoo in Haiti and even investigated the practice of devil worship out of sheer curiosity.

Her own psychic abilities were naturally called into question by the scientific community and the sceptics. In 1931, she agreed to be tested for her alleged

Eileen Garrett, founder of the Parapsychology Foundation.

ability to leave her body while in a trance and report on distant scenes that she had seen while in her astral state. In an apartment in New York, a psychiatrist and a secretary watched while Garrett fell into a trance, with the specific intention of trying to see what was going on in a doctor's surgery in Reykjavik, Iceland. The doctor in Iceland had placed several items on a table in his office, and Garrett was to describe them to the psychiatrist in New York.

The results of that experiment are still startling today. Garrett successfully described all the items on the table. She then went on to read a passage from the book that the doctor in Reykjavik was reading, word for word, and to tell the psychiatrist that the doctor's head was bandaged for some reason. The doctor later confirmed that she had indeed quoted the book exactly, and that because of a minor accident just before the experiment started, he had indeed bandaged his head. He also reported sensing Garrett's presence in the room at the time of the experiment.

Garrett travelled the world to lecture on psychic phenomena, and was often asked to conduct séances. These were usually very small, private affairs, not the theatrical shows so often associated with mediums, and Garrett never charged a penny for her services in the fifty years that she performed her séances. One such séance took place in London on 7 October 1930, under the auspices of Harry Price, director of the National Laboratory of Psychic Research. There were two other people present in the séance room: Miss Ethel Beenham, Price's secretary, and Ian Coster, an Australian newspaper reporter. Two days before the séance took place, the British airship, the R-101 had famously crashed in northern France during its maiden voyage; all but six of the fifty-four people on board had died in the disaster. Three months prior to the séance, Sir Arthur Conan Doyle, a famous believer in the spirit world, had died, and Coster, sensing a great story for his paper, asked Garrett to contact him.

As the séance began, Garrett fell into a trance. No sooner had she closed her eyes than she began to weep, and start talking excitedly about the R-101 crash. Garrett was channelling the spirit of Flight Lieutenant Irwin, the commander of the R-101, and provided considerable technical detail which was beyond her own knowledge: "The whole bulk of the dirigible was . . . too much for her engine capacity . . . Useful lift too small . . . elevator jammed . . . Oil pipe plugged". When Irwin left Garrett, Conan Doyle allegedly did make an appearance, but those present at the séance were more fascinated by the account given by Irwin. Price took a copy of the transcript of the séance to the R-101's builders at the Royal Airship Works in Cardington, where it was passed on to a man named Charlton, an acclaimed expert on the R-101. Charlton declared that he was amazed by the accuracy of the transcript, by the technical information and the revelations about the secret details of the airship.

The R-101 séance gained Garrett instant fame as a medium, but she was not only capable of channelling the spirits. She could also see things that were happening at a distance, or even in the future. One evening during World War I, Garrett was dining with friends at the exclusive Savoy Hotel in London. She suddenly felt herself surrounded by reeking fumes and the sounds of mortar shells and gunfire. At the same time, she experienced a clairvoyant vision of her husband being blown up on a battlefield. A few days later, she received a letter from the War Office, telling her that her husband had not returned from a reconnaissance mission, and was presumed dead.

Despite her amazing powers, Garrett herself remained a sceptic throughout her life. The main reason that she founded the Parapsychology Foundation was to find answers as to why she had these amazing powers, and she felt certain that one day science would provide those answers: "any attempt to explain the psyche and its manifold patterns in terms of language gets bogged down. The answer may well come from other aspects of science as yet not heard from officially."

Garrett remained dubious about the origins of her powers right up to her death in 1970. In her autobiography, she acknowledged that the spirits she communicated with might well have been manifestations from her own subconscious. She explained that her powers of clairvoyance, telepathy and remote viewing were nothing supernatural or paranormal, and speculated that they might have been generated by the hypothalamus gland in her brain. The truth is, she did have those powers. Where they came from is another question. Perhaps the foundation she dedicated much of her life to will one day find the answers, perhaps not.

Sai Baba

Another of the great showmen among psychics, Sai Baba claims to be able to raise the dead, heal the sick and produce religious artefacts and food out of thin air. The miracles of Sai Baba are so incredible that they seem beyond belief. Yet the countless number of witnesses who have come forward to testify to his astonishing powers have come from all walks of life, including government officials, religious leaders and scientists.

When he was born on 23 November 1926, under the name of Satyanarayana Raju, he appeared to be a normal, healthy Indian child, but his special abilities quickly became recognized. At school, for example, he soon became extremely popular due to his uncanny ability to produce sweets from an empty bag! But it was a strange incident that happened to him when he was thirteen that proved to be the turning point in Satyanarayana's life. While walking home from school with friends, he suddenly screamed and fell to the ground, holding his right foot. Everyone thought that he had been bitten by a scorpion, but the following day he showed no sign of pain or sickness, until in the evening he suddenly fell unconscious to the ground. Satyanarayana recovered the following day, but he seemed to be a completely different person. He would unexpectedly burst into song or recite long passages in Sanskrit that were way beyond anything he had been taught. His parents consulted various doctors, all to no avail.

One morning while working with his father, he called the rest of his family together. He waved his hand in front of them and produced sweets and flowers, seemingly out of thin air. The news of Satyanarayana's conjuring tricks soon spread, and his father became extremely angry. He told his son, "This is too much! It must stop! What are you? Tell me – a ghost, a god, or a madcap?" Baba replied, without flinching, "I am Sai Baba. I have come to ward off your troubles; keep your houses clean and pure." The Raju family had never heard of anyone by the name of Sai Baba, but other people in their village had. Sai Baba was a Hindu holy man who performed many miracles, including healing the sick with ash from a fire which he kept eternally burning at a mosque. He had died in 1918, but he told his followers that he would be reborn. Was Satyanarayana the new incarnation of Sai Baba? Naturally, everyone was pretty sceptical about that, thinking Satyanarayana a fool. Eventually, of course, he was directly challenged: if he truly were the incarnation of Sai Baba, then he must prove it to them. He asked his sceptical townsman to pass him some jasmine flowers. Then he threw them on to the floor, and to the amazement of everyone, they landed in such a way as to spell out "Sai Baba".

In time, Satyanarayana came to meet with devotees of Sai Baba who worshipped at his mosque, and he felt that he recognized them. On one occasion, he took a photograph from someone, looked at it, and named the person in the picture, even though he had never met him. But to most people who have been touched by Satyanarayana's incredible powers, it doesn't matter if he is the reincarnation of Sai Baba or not. What really matters are his awesome abilities. He is well known for producing holy ash out of nowhere, sometimes scooped from the air and sprinkled on to the hands of visitors, or alternatively poured out of an empty urn. He claims that this holy ash has a variety of uses, and it is believed to have cured many illnesses. But it is his power to produce more solid objects out of thin air that has attracted the most attention. He is able to produce pretty much anything that anyone asks of him, seemingly from another dimension.

The author of *Sai Baba, Man of Miracles*, wrote of an occasion when he interviewed the mystic. Sai Baba asked Howard Murphet what the year of his birth was and then said that he would produce for him an American coin minted in that year:

> *"He began to circle his down-turned hand in the air in front of us, making perhaps half a dozen small circles, saying the while 'It's coming now . . . coming . . . here it is!' Then he closed his hand and held it before me, smiling as if enjoying my eager expectancy. When the coin dropped from his hand to mine, I noticed first that it was heavy and golden. On closer examination I found, to my delight, that it was a genuine milled American ten-dollar coin, with the year of my birth stamped beneath a profile head of the Statue of Liberty."*

His power to produce items out of thin air is hard to believe. As hard to believe as the many miracles performed by Jesus Christ, which are taken for granted by millions of Christians as fact. Sai Baba sees himself in the same vein as Christ – a holy man sent to Earth on a mission. His ability to make things appear from nowhere is to him a very small part of his work, and a minor and insignificant part at that.

With such a phenomenon, there will always be

sceptics, but Sai Baba has puzzled even them. One Australian sceptic decided to test the man. He knew that every Rolex watch has an individual serial number on it, and he asked Sai Baba to materialize one for him. The guru did so with a wave of his hand. When he returned to Australia, the sceptic used the serial number to trace when and where the watch had been bought. He went to the shop, and asked the owner if he could remember who had bought the watch and when. The proprietor remembered it very well, for the person who had bought it stood out from his usual customers. It was an Indian gentleman, dressed in orange, with strange, fuzzy hair. That was an exact description of Sai Baba. As to the date the watch was bought, the shop owner kept meticulous records. It transpired that the watch had been bought at the exact time that Sai Baba had materialized it for the Australian. Both he and the watch must have been in two places at the same time.

To many followers of Sai Baba, it is his healing abilities which are to be celebrated above all others. There are countless stories of how he has cured the sick. One such is the tale of a sixty-year-old factory worker who visited Sai Baba in 1953, in the hope of finding a cure for severe gastric ulcers that were making his life a misery. He was given a room, and told to wait for a visit from the mystic. When Sai Baba came to see him, he made absolutely no attempt to cure him, and he just laughed when the gentleman said that he would rather die than go on suffering. Sai Baba then left the room without another word.

Eventually the man's condition deteriorated and he fell into a coma. When Sai Baba learned of this, he told the man's wife not to worry, that everything would be just fine. The next day there was still no improvement, so the man's wife sent for a nurse. The nurse said that the man was so close to death that there was no way of saving him. An hour later he became very cold, and his family reported that they had heard a death rattle in his throat. Slowly he turned blue and rigor mortis set in. When the family reported this to Sai Baba, he laughed again and told them not to worry. He went to the man's room to see his condition, and then left once more without saying a word.

Three days later, the body of the man looked decidedly like a corpse. It was dark, cold and smelled of decomposition. The family were advised that the man was dead and that he should be buried, but Sai Baba replied to them that they should have no fear, the man would be all right. The following day, Sai Baba went to the man's room once more, and found the family sitting there looking distraught. He asked them to leave, and remained with the body for a few minutes. Then he opened the door and called the family back in. To their utter relief, joy and amazement, they found the "dead" man conscious, smiling and sitting up in bed! The next day he was well enough to walk. When he went to hospital, it was found that his gastric ulcers had vanished – they never returned.

Another astounding story concerns an Australian who visited Sai Baba in the hope and belief that he could cure his wife of terminal cancer. His wife had been written off by the medical profession as untreatable due to the nature of her disease, and so he turned to the mystic as his last hope. His meeting with Sai Baba was all too brief. When they met, Sai Baba simply said to him, "You shouldn't be here. Your wife needs you. She will be well." He then tapped the Australian on the forehead three times. The man vanished in front of a large crowd of people, all of whom have testified to the event, and then reappeared beside his wife's hospital bed in Australia. She made a full recovery. Naturally, the Australian was somewhat baffled by the experience, and he checked his passport. It was correctly stamped with that day's date, showing that he had re-entered Australia, yet only seconds before he had been in India.

As unbelievable as these and many other such stories are, Sai Baba dismissed these "miracles" as the least important part of his work. He claims that "miracles are my visiting cards", but his mission is to attract attention to his spiritual teachings – to lead humanity away from violence and hatred towards compassion and higher consciousness. He explains it this way: "I give you what you want in order that you may want what I have come to give." He claims that if we all embrace the spiritual principle of unconditional love then we too can become a godlike being and will develop similar psychic powers. This is, he asserts, the next evolutionary step of humankind. However, Sai Baba has also said that this will not be achieved in his lifetime. He has already said that he will be reborn as Prema Sai in the twenty-first century in order to complete his work.

Scientists, and sceptics such as James Randi, point to the fact that Sai Baba has never been tested by researchers in any way, let alone under laboratory conditions. India's leading debunker of psychics, B. Premanand, claims to be able to duplicate all of Sai Baba's "tricks", and tours the world demonstrating how they are done. However, even he had no rational explanation for the stories mentioned above, other than that the people are obviously lying. But why should so many people who claim to have witnessed Sai Baba's powers fabricate these incredible stories? Why should Sai Baba create the myth about himself, if not for money? These are questions to which I have no answers. I only know that Sai Baba devotes his life to helping others. He has built an ultra-modern 300-bed hospital which performs highly specialized operations. There is absolutely no charge to the patients for professional or hospital expenses. Recently, he initiated a project to provide an adequate supply of pure water to 1.5 million inhabitants of the State of Andhra Pradesh in India who were living in drought conditions. This is Sai Baba's way of demonstrating one of his teachings: that it is the duty of society to ensure that all people have access to the basic requirements for the sustenance of human life.

He is indeed a truly mystifying phenomenon. Depending upon your point of view, he is either the greatest psychic ever to have lived; the reincarnation of a Hindu holy man with the power to generate miracles; or the most convincing magician and liar ever to have walked the planet. Whichever he truly is, he has baffled many of the greatest scientific minds for the best part of half a century.

Doris Stokes

Doris Stokes has been hailed as perhaps the greatest medium of the twentieth century. In her lifetime, she always came across as a perfectly ordinary, down-to-earth person, but she had a special gift. Doris was a medium who claimed to be able to hear the dead speak – an ability known as clairaudience.

When Doris appeared on the *Don Lane Show* in Australia, she became an overnight sensation. The network's switchboard was flooded with calls, letters poured in, and Channel 9 took off one of their most popular programmes at the time to make room for a second, hour-long programme about her. Doris had a huge impact on the Australian viewers, but by no means for her abilities as a showperson. She came across as a very ordinary woman with an extraordinary gift, something which is unusual in the field of psychic powers. A great many mediums who have achieved television success rely on creating a spooky atmosphere to sell themselves, but Doris was something different.

In the television studio, her down-to-earth, good-humoured manner soon saw to it that there was nothing "spooky" about her performance. All she did was to stand in front of the audience and wait for the voices to give her information. But the information that she gave was astounding in its accuracy. On one occasion, she pointed to one of Don Lane's guests and said, "That lady over there. I've got a man here called Bert."

"That's my brother-in-law," the amazed woman replied.

"He says he went over very quickly."

"That's right."

"Who's Wyn?"

"I'm Wyn."

The curious thing about Doris Stokes was that the information that she gave was usually just as trivial as that – a simple message from a deceased relative, not a prediction of the end of the world. But the accuracy of the names and details that she gave left her recipients in no doubt that they were witnessing a paranormal phenomenon.

Doris's psychic powers manifested themselves from an early age, when she found herself describing, or predicting, things that she could not have known by normal means. Her mother was very worried by this, but she was encouraged by her father, who was himself a psychic. But it was not until her father died and Doris was married that her powers reached their full potential, and her experiences left her in no doubt that she was in fact in touch with the dead.

The experience which touched Doris the most happened during World War II, after her husband had been reported missing in action. Doris visited a local Spiritualist church, and a medium at the church confirmed that her husband was dead. She returned home to her baby son in a state of shock and distress, but what happened next confirmed her feelings that her husband was still alive:

> "Then the bedroom door flew open so sharply I thought it was mother bursting in and there stood my father. My mouth dropped open. He looked as real and as solid as he did when he was alive. The years rolled back and I was thirteen again.
>
> 'Dad?' I whispered.

> *'I never lied to you, did I, Doll?' he asked.*
> *'I don't think so,' I said.*
> *'I'm not lying to you now. John is not with us and on Christmas Day you will have proof of this.'*
> *Then as I watched, he vanished."*

Three days later, Doris received an official letter from the War Office, telling her that John was dead, and that as soon as the grave numbers were sorted out, they would inform her of where he was buried. While all John's friends and relatives began the process of mourning his death, Doris refused to believe it. She was convinced that she had received a message from the other side, from her father, telling her that John was still alive. On Christmas Day, Doris rushed downstairs to greet the postgirl. There was just the one letter that day, once more from the War Office. The letter confirmed what the spirit of Doris's father had said. John was suffering from head injuries which had caused him temporary blindness, and he was recovering in a prisoner of war camp in Holland. He was very much alive.

Doris's father visited her on one other occasion, this time with news of a different nature. Shortly after she received the news that her husband was alive and recovering, Doris was bathing her baby son, John Michael. Suddenly, she froze and felt the back of her neck begin to prickle. Then she heard a soft voice telling her, "He's done his time on Earth. He's got to come back to spirit." Doris knew instantly that the voice was talking about her son. She fabricated an illness for him in order to get him thoroughly checked out at her local hospital. She then cancelled the appointment, thinking that something might happen to him in hospital. One night, while putting her son to bed, Doris suddenly felt a presence in the room. She turned around and saw her father once again, standing in the doorway, and he confirmed her fears:

> *"Doll, you know this isn't right. John Michael should be with us. He has to come back. At quarter to three next Friday I'll come for him and you must hand him over to me. Don't worry. I'll take good care of him."*

Her father then vanished, leaving Doris beside herself with anguish. John Michael became a little unwell, and Doris called for the doctor, who told her that he was suffering from a cold and that she shouldn't worry. His condition deteriorated, and Doris continually called the doctor who thought that she was simply being melodramatic and refused to visit her. Eventually, Doris called the doctor one last time and threatened that if he did not come, she would take her baby to the police station. The doctor sent out a locum, who took one look at the baby and decided that he needed to go straight to the hospital.

On the Friday morning, Doris called in at the doctor's surgery on her way to the hospital to see her son. She was sitting in the waiting room when a cleaning girl popped her head round the door and asked if a Mrs Stokes was there, because a policeman had come to see her. The policeman told her that she had to come to the hospital straight away because her son had taken a turn for the worse. At the hospital, Doris sat beside her son's bed for hours, watching him slowly fade away. She picked him up and held him in her arms, and looked down lovingly at his frail body:

". . . when I raised my head, my father was standing on the other side of the cot. He didn't say a word. He looked steadily at me and then silently held out his hands. I clutched John Michael more tightly, but still my father held out his hands. There was a long pause. I just didn't have a choice. Slowly, reluctantly, I passed my baby across, and at the very instant father took my son in his arms, I looked down and saw my little John Michael was dead."

When Doris looked up again, her father was gone. She took a look at the ward clock, and saw that it was just after quarter to three.

At the time that Doris appeared on the *Don Lane Show*, there was another man in town, a man with a reputation for debunking fake psychics. Over breakfast, Doris liked to listen to Bert Newton on Australian radio, and one morning she tuned in to hear his guest of the day, James Randi, being interviewed. What transpired must have been a dream come true for the radio network. Randi said that it was his mission in life to expose fakes such as Uri Geller and Doris Stokes. He said that he could duplicate Geller's spoon-bending by normal magic trickery, and as for Stokes, he claimed that she was taking the Australian people for a ride. He said that he had seen Doris performing in London and was convinced even then that she was a fake.

Doris was incensed by the accusation, especially as she had no knowledge of ever performing a sitting when he was present. She called the radio network and asked to be put on air to answer her critic. The broadcast went as follows:

"Now, Mr Randi," said Stokes, "I might not be there in body but I'm there in spirit. You can say to me what you have to say."

"Yes, all right," replied Randi. "You're conning the people of Australia."

"You are saying the Australian people are fools, then?"

"No, I didn't say that."

"By implication you did, because I was here in 1978 and I am back again now, so if I'm conning the people they must be a pack of fools to be taken in twice . . . Look, there's a quick way out of this, Mr Randi. You say I'm a fake. Well if I'm a fake it's possible to duplicate what I do. Now, I'm doing a meeting on Thursday evening at Dallasbrook Hall so I challenge you to come on stage with me and I'll do my thing with the audience – faking you call it – and then you fake it in the same way and we'll let the audience make up their own minds."

Doris had thrown down the gauntlet, but Randi refused the invitation, claiming that he had more important things to do. Doris was not to be put off:

"But you said you wanted to expose fakes! Surely there's nothing more important than that? By the way, when did you say you saw me in London?"

"January."

"January this year?" Doris asked.

"That's right."

Now Doris knew that she could expose Randi as a liar. In January of that year, she had not given a single sitting; she had been in hospital undergoing a hysterectomy.

> *"Well, it must have been my spirit body you saw then, son, because I was in hospital having a major operation and I've got documents to prove it."*
>
> *". . . Oh dear, is that the time?" said Randi, "I'd love to go on but I've got another appointment and my taxi's ticking away outside."*

Doris had debunked the debunker. But Randi is not one to take defeat lightly. In his book, *An Encyclopedia of Claims, Frauds and Hoaxes of the Occult and Supernatural*, the entry for "Stokes, Doris" reads as follows:

> *"Primarily as a clairaudient, UK psychic performer Ms Stokes became very popular in Australia in the 1980s. Her techniques were essentially cold reading, though she also depended on obtaining information in person in advance from her clients, who were then encouraged to show up at her public performances, at which time the information could be given back to them as if received psychically from the Great Beyond."*

Randi's claim in this "definition" of Doris Stokes comes from an admission that Doris made in her book, *Voices*. In her youth, when Doris first started to perform her talents in front of an audience, she would often find that the voices that came to her would fade, leaving awkward silences. She was young and felt very special because of her psychic powers, and was therefore prone to showing off. So when the voices stopped, she followed the advice of another medium. He told her to get to her meetings early and listen to the conversations of the audience, where she would be bound to pick up a few hints, names and dates. That way, if the voices went silent, she could simply make up the messages, leaving the audience happy.

Doris admitted to using this technique on two occasions. On one of those two occasions, she made some notes from the conversations that she had overheard from the audience, and slipped them into her hymn book. During her performance, the voices suddenly stopped in the middle of a message for a lady in the audience, and Doris fumbled for her notes, but could not find them. She tried to make something up from memory, but noticed that the lady seemed somewhat bewildered by what she had said. Just as abruptly as the voices had left her, they returned. Doris managed two real messages, but then became aware that her spirit guide had taken over and was saying, "Now we'll get back to Mrs X and you'll apologise to her and tell her that the last part of the message didn't come from the spirit world." Doris confessed to the lady, and promised herself that she would never cheat again.

Even with this admission, does Doris deserve the definition given her by James Randi? She has passed away, and cannot answer her critic as she did in Australia. I think that Doris would be content to be judged by the results of her work, and they speak for themselves. Whether charlatan or not, she brought comfort to thousands of people.

Uri Geller

Uri Geller was born in Israel on 20 December 1946. His parents are of Hungarian and Austrian descent, and on his mother's side he is distantly related to the father of psychology, Sigmund Freud. Geller's powers began to manifest themselves when he was a small child: he found that he was able to read his mother's mind, could affect the workings of clocks and watches simply by looking at them, and cause spoons and forks to bend or break. At first his parents were a bit embarrassed by the extraordinary things that Uri was capable of, but eventually became concerned and even considered consulting a psychiatrist.

By the age of six, Uri realized he could read his mother's mind. She came back from a party where she had been playing cards, and Uri was able to tell exactly how much money she had won just by looking at her. But at this early age, he had little control over his powers. When he first went to school, his father gave him a watch, but it never seemed to work properly. One day, Uri stared at the watch, and to his amazement, the hands started to spin furiously; Uri began to suspect that it was something to do with him rather than the watch. In a restaurant with his parents, his soup spoon suddenly broke in two, and spoons and forks on nearby tables began to bend, again not by his will, but by a power over which he had little control. By the time he reached thirteen, however, Uri had become a master of his powers, not they of him. He learned to cheat at school exams by reading the minds of others in his class. He said that he only had to stare at the backs of their heads to "see" the answers.

Geller began giving demonstrations of his powers in 1968, first to groups of schoolchildren and at private parties, then to larger audiences in theatres all over Israel. By the summer of 1971, he had become something of a pop icon to teenagers of Israel; he was young, tall, good-looking and his shows were like nothing they had ever seen before. On stage, Geller would repair broken watches just by looking at them, bend spoons by gently massaging them with his finger and break metal hoops without even touching them – the youth of Israel just loved this new age "magician".

News of Uri's talent soon spread, and came to the attention of an American psychical investigator, Andrija Puharich, who flew to Israel to see Geller for himself. Geller was performing a show at a disco in Jaffa on 17 August 1971, and Puharich was in the audience, watching him very closely. The first thing that Puharich observed was that Geller obviously loved performing for an audience – he was a born showman. Puharich watched with a sceptical eye. He had seen many magicians demonstrating their trickery on stage before, and he knew the difference between an illusion and a psychic power. He was unimpressed when Geller put on a blindfold and asked members of the audience to write words on a blackboard. Sure, he guessed right every time, but Puharich knew that this could easily be done by having a few paid friends in the audience. The last feat that Geller performed, however, caught Puharich's attention, and made him want to know more. Uri announced to the audience that he would break a ring without touching it, and a woman in the audience offered her ring for the performance. She showed it to the audience, then Uri told her to hold it tightly in her hand. He then placed his own hand above hers and held it there for a few seconds. When she opened her hand, the ring had snapped clean in two.

Geller had steadfastly refused to be tested by anyone, but after the show Puharich asked him if he would submit to a few scientific tests the next day. For some reason Uri agreed, and he flew to New York with Puharich the following day. The first display of his powers convinced Puharich that he was a genuine psychic. Geller placed a notepad on the table, then asked Puharich to think of three numbers. Puharich chose 4, 3 and 2. Geller then asked him to turn the notepad over. On the other side Puharich saw the numbers 4, 3 and 2, which Geller had written down before he had even thought of the numbers. Puharich was convinced that Geller had telepathically influenced him into choosing these three numbers.

Geller gave several demonstrations for Puharich. He raised the temperature of a thermometer just by staring at it, bent a stream of water issuing from a tap by placing his finger near it and made a compass needle move by concentrating on it. Puharich now firmly believed that Uri was a true psychic with the power of psychokinesis. He thought that he had made the scientific find of the century – a genuine psychic who could perform even under laboratory conditions, and whose powers could be called upon at will. On 1 December 1971, Puharich decided to hypnotize Geller, in the hope of discovering the origin of his powers. This hypnotism session led Puharich to write a book, *Uri: A Journal of the Mystery of Uri Geller*, which described what happened while Uri was "under". The events of that day are almost beyond belief.

Puharich regressed Uri to his childhood, and asked him where he was. He replied that he was in a cave in Cyprus, which was where his family lived when he was thirteen, and that he was learning "about people who come from space". He then added that he was not allowed to talk further about this. Uri was then taken back further, and began to speak in Hebrew, his first language. In Hebrew, he described an event which had happened when he was three years old. He was in a garden in Tel Aviv, and saw a shining object floating in the air above his head, while a ringing noise sounded in the air. As the object moved closer to him, he became bathed in light and fainted. While Uri was relating these events, Puharich and the other investigators in the room heard a voice which seemed to come from above their heads. Puharich described it as "unearthly and metallic". The voice said, "It was we who found Uri in the garden when he was three. He is our helper, sent to help man. We programmed him in the garden." The voice went on to explain that the world was on the brink of war, and that Uri had been programmed to avert the extinction of the human race.

When Uri came out of the hypnotic trance, he had no memory of any of this, so Puharich played back a recording of the session. When the metallic voice came over the speaker, Uri grabbed the cassette from the recorder, and Puharich watched as it disappeared. How convenient, the sceptics have said, that the only evidence of the session should mysteriously vanish, but the metallic voice appeared numerous times afterwards.

On several occasions, the mysterious entities tried to convince Puharich of their existence. They made his car engine stop and then start again; they "teleported" his briefcase from his house in New York to his apartment in Tel Aviv. When Uri and Puharich visited an army base, they were followed by a red light in the sky that only they, and not their military escort, could see. On 4 November 1972, Geller was travelling by jet from London to Munich, when his camera suddenly rose into the air of its own accord, and stopped in front of him as if signalling for him to take a picture. Uri could see nothing except the clouds, but took several photographs. When the film was developed, five of the photographs contained images which Geller, and many others, believe to be UFOs alongside the plane.

The events became even stranger. A few years prior to meeting Uri Geller, Puharich himself had received messages from some mysterious beings who called themselves the "Nine", and who claimed to come from outer space. During one of his sessions with Geller, Puharich asked the metallic voice if it was one of the Nine, and it replied that it was. The voice told Puharich that the Nine were beings from another dimension, and that they lived in a starship called *Spectra*, which had been watching Earth for thousands of years. They would soon make their presence known by landing on the Earth.

The whole thing sounds so absurd that it is very easy to dismiss. Any tape recordings of the voice mysteriously disappeared. Geller could simply have thrown his own voice during the sittings, and then made the cassettes disappear by sleight of hand. How he could have made Puharich's briefcase mysteriously transport itself from New York to Tel Aviv is distinctly harder to explain, although only two people testify to this – Geller and Puharich. But Geller himself has said that he does not believe that he has been chosen by the "Nine" to be their messenger on Earth. He has publicly declared that the events described by Puharich leave him utterly dumbfounded, and that he is unable to offer an explanation. So is Puharich the one trying to "pull the wool over our eyes"? The answer must be itself a question: why would he? Puharich went to Tel Aviv to test Uri Geller's powers as a psychic, not as a messenger from another dimension. His sole aim was to prove that Geller possessed paranormal powers, and surely a lot of nonsense about aliens would undermine his own credibility?

In fact, that was exactly what happened. Geller was becoming very worried by the events at Puharich's laboratory. At the time, he was not interested in proving scientifically that he had amazing powers, and certainly had no desire to establish the existence of aliens. He simply wanted fame and money, and in June 1972 he flew to Munich to tour under the guidance of a professional impresario, Yasha Katz. Puharich was left behind in New York.

Katz was incredibly good at his job. He made sure that Uri was greeted by a crowd of reporters, and one of them asked Uri, "What can you do that would be really astounding? . . . How about stopping a cable car in mid-air?" Geller thought that he was up to the challenge, and the crowd of reporters followed him to a mountain resort near Munich. As one of the cable cars left for the top of the mountain, Geller concentrated hard, but nothing happened. It went up and down the mountain normally, and the reporters soon started to lose interest. Suddenly, just as the reporters were turning away, the cable car stopped. The mechanic who was standing by radioed the control centre and was told that the main switch had suddenly flipped off for no apparent reason. The reporters telephoned their editors, and Uri Geller took his first steps on the world stage.

Uri toured Germany for several weeks, his fame steadily growing. Offers flooded in, and there was even talk of him appearing in a musical about psychic powers. After weeks of unrelenting exposure, his popularity began to fade, and it seemed that he might be in danger of becoming a passing fad. At this point, Uri returned to America, where Puharich had arranged for him to be tested by some of America's leading scientists.

Uri was constantly surrounded by eminent scientists, of whom he was initially very suspicious. He knew that their remit was to prove him a fraud, not to prove him a genuine psychic, but he went along with their tests. Dr Werhner von Braun, the inventor of the V-2 rocket, was among those who witnessed Uri's powers at the time. In von Braun's office, Uri flattened von Braun's gold wedding ring while von Braun was holding it. Then von Braun discovered that his calculator battery was flat. Geller held the calculator in his hands, and when von Braun turned it on again, the battery was working, and the display flashed random numbers. After the experiments, Dr von Braun stated, "Geller has bent the ring in the palm of my hand without ever touching it. Personally I have no scientific explanation for the phenomena."

Geller underwent a series of rigorous tests at the Stanford Research Institute in California, conducted by Dr Hal Puthoff and Russell Targ. Uri was first asked to bend a brass ring out of shape, while a television monitor silently watched. Every time that Uri concentrated on the ring, the monitor began to distort and, at the same time, a computer on the floor below Uri began to malfunction.

The next series of tests were intended to establish whether he had ESP or not. A die was placed in a closed box and then shaken. Uri was asked by the scientists what was shown on the top of the die. He guessed right every single time. He was also right when asked to predict which of ten empty cans sitting on a table was covering a small object. The results of the Puthoff and Targ experiments were published in the British journal *Nature*, and following Geller's achievements, the two scientists had this to say:

> *"As a result of Geller's success in this experimental period, we consider that he has demonstrated his paranormal, perceptual ability in a convincing and unambiguous manner."*

So Uri had convinced some of the great scientific minds of America that he was a genuine psychic. But unknown to him Nemesis was waiting, in the form of the magician James Randi, the most celebrated illusionist since Harry Houdini, and the greatest sceptic of all things paranormal.

Uri was asked to appear at the offices of *Time* magazine, and did so on 6 February 1973. At the offices, he met with some hostility from two *Time* editors and two stage magicians, Charles Reynolds and James Randi, the man who was determined to prove that Geller was a fake. He was soon set to the test, and performed admirably. He succeeded in demonstrating his telepathic powers by duplicating a drawing in a sealed envelope. He bent a fork by stroking it lightly; the fork continued to bend after he had put it down. Charles Reynolds gave Uri his own house key to bend, and again Uri successfully did so.

He left the offices of *Time* magazine confident that he had proved himself once more. The article which the magazine published a few weeks later was, however, damning. In the article, Charles Reynolds and James Randi claimed that they could easily duplicate every one of Uri's "tricks", and that Randi had in fact done so after Uri had left the offices. The article concluded by stating that Geller had been forced to leave Israel in disgrace after he had been accused of fraud. That was a direct assault on Uri, based entirely on a libellous untruth. Uri has successfully sued Randi several times since then. The article, though now considered to be woefully biased against Uri Geller, and just plain lies, did at the time harm his reputation in America. The public simply dismissed him as just another trickster, and he moved to Britain to demonstrate his talents on the European stage once more.

Geller turned overnight into the most controversial man in Britain after he appeared on the *David Dimbleby Talk-in* on the BBC on 23 November 1973. During the show he bent a fork which Dimbleby held in his own hand, started two broken watches by rubbing them and caused the hands of one of them to bend upwards. He even made a fork on the end of a table bend of its own accord. At the end of the television programme, the producer came on to announce that the station had received dozens of calls from viewers who claimed that their own cutlery had mysteriously started to bend. Geller became an overnight sensation, and the excitement experienced in Britain was reported all over the world. Even the Americans who had not taken him seriously while he was there suddenly started to see him as the man of the moment.

The *People* newspaper decided to get in on the act. They announced that at midday on the Sunday following the *David Dimbleby Talk-in*, Uri would concentrate his powers and try to make cutlery bend all over England. The newspaper asked its readers to report any such phenomena to the editor. Shortly after noon that day, the newspaper received a flood of calls declaring not only that cutlery all over the country had mysteriously bent, but that many people's watches had suddenly started working again. Uri Geller finally achieved what he always hoped for – fame and money.

Just two days after the Dimbleby programme, Geller demonstrated his powers in Paris; he moved on to perform amazing feats throughout the whole of Europe and Scandinavia, before being once more tested by scientists, again with astonishing results.

After testing Uri, Professor David Bohn and Professor John Hasted of Birkbeck College, London, announced:

> "We feel that if similar tests are made later, enough instances of this kind will probably accumulate, so that there will be no room for reasonable doubt that some new process is involved here, which cannot be accounted for or explained in terms of the present known laws of physics. Indeed, we already feel that we have gone some distance towards this point."

Professor P. Plum of the University of Copenhagen was even more emphatic. He believed that Uri Geller had single-handedly proved the existence of psychic phenomena:

"Uri Geller, as a psychic genius, has been able to demonstrate the repeatability of controlled scientific psychic experiments. Thereby he has proved the reality of psychic phenomena (such as telekinesis, clairvoyance and telepathy)."

Geller went on to achieve international fame and to become one of the best-known psychics in the world. He has been rigorously tested throughout his career, under very strict laboratory conditions, and the conclusion of the scientific community is that he is not a fraud. If not a fraud, then he must have genuine psychic ability. There are many sceptics out there, however, who still refuse to hear the evidence that some of the greatest scientific minds have accumulated over the years, the most prominent of whom remains James Randi.

Ever since Randi first "set up" Geller back in the 1970s, the two have had an ongoing feud. Randi believes that Geller is a fraud, and that he himself is capable of repeating any of Geller's amazing feats using simple trickery. One investigator decided to take Randi up on the challenge. When Colin Wilson, author of *The Geller Phenomenon*, met James Randi, Randi showed an ability to bend spoons and even made Wilson's watch go back several hours just by rubbing it. He was not, however, able to perform any of Geller's mind-reading abilities.

On 12 April 1999, Uri Geller saw James Randi

standing outside the cordoned area where magician David Blane was buried. Uri was with his wife, their two children and his brother-in-law, Shipi. Shipi filmed the meeting on a camcorder. Uri walked over to James Randi, who was just a few feet away, and extended his hand in greeting. Randi refused to shake his hand, and when Uri asked why, Randi replied, "because I hate your guts". What can be read into this statement? Does Randi despise Uri so much because he has been unable, in nearly thirty years, to expose him as a fraud? Quite possibly.

I leave the investigation into this amazing psychic with a quote by Dr Kit Pedler, Head of the Electron Microscopy Department at the University of London, shortly after he witnessed Geller's powers for himself:

> *"A scientist would have to be either massively ignorant or a confirmed bigot to deny the evidence that the human mind can make connection with space, time and matter in ways which have nothing to do with the ordinary senses. Further, he cannot deny that these connections are compatible with current thinking in physics, and may in the future become accepted as a part of an extended science in which the description 'paranormal' no longer applies, and can be replaced by 'normal'."*

Edgar Cayce

Edgar Cayce became the most documented prophet of our time, and gained fame under the nickname of the "Sleeping Prophet". He was born in 1877 on a farm near Hopkinsville, Kentucky. Evidence of his amazing talents came to the fore when he was young, and he found that he was able to master his studies at school simply by sleeping on the relevant textbook. The information contained within the book would somehow be absorbed into his head, and it is believed that this is where he gained his nickname.

For most of his adult life, Cayce was able to provide intuitive insights into nearly any question imaginable. When people came to him with a question, he would place himself into a sleep-induced trance-like state. While in that state, he could respond to virtually any question asked. His responses came to be called "readings", and today those readings constitute one of the largest and most impressive records of intuitive information to emanate from a single individual.

At the age of twenty-one, Cayce developed a gradual throat paralysis which threatened the permanent loss of his voice. When doctors were unable to find a cause for his condition, he entered the same hypnotic sleep that he had used to learn his school lessons years before. In that state, he was able to recommend a cure which successfully repaired his throat muscles and restored his voice to normal. He soon discovered that he could use the same technique to help heal others. During the 1920s and 1930s, long before traditional medicine became interested in the effects that the mind can have over the body, Edgar Cayce was laying the groundwork for one of the most fascinating truths in medical history – namely that what one thinks and feels emotionally will find expression in the physical body. Cayce believed that the mind was a powerful tool in creating health and well-being. He was ahead of his time – it was to be several decades before medical science would investigate the idea that mental patterns could have a direct impact upon physical health and disease.

Cayce's turning point as a psychic came when he was just thirteen years old. He was on the farm in Kentucky, where he grew up, engaged in a favourite pastime of his – reading the Bible. He suddenly became aware of the fact that he was not alone, and looked up to see a woman standing before him. The sun was shining behind her, and at first he couldn't see who she was, and assumed that the figure was his mother. But when she spoke, he did not recognize her voice, which appeared to be uncannily soft and lyrical. The figure simply said to him, "Your prayers have been answered. Tell me what you would like most of all, so that I may give it to you." Stunned by the presence of the woman, Cayce stammered out that what he wanted most of all was to be able to help others, especially children, when they were sick. The figure did not reply, and vanished into the brilliant light of the sun behind her. Edgar returned to his reading of the Bible, somewhat bemused. He initially thought that the vision was a manifestation of his own mind, and that he might be on the verge of going mad. Soon after the vision, however, he began to receive signs that he had been given special powers. He had never been particularly bright as a student, his teachers complaining that he was inattentive and a dreamer. This was much to the consternation of his father, who wished Edgar could excel at school, and was constantly dismayed when he did not. The night after his vision, Edgar was studying his spelling primer, without much success, when his father decided to take matters into his own hands. The two of them sat at the table with the book between them, and over the course of the evening, the father spoke one word after another, and Edgar spelled the majority of them incorrectly. At half past ten that evening, Edgar heard the same voice as in the vision saying, "If you can sleep a little, we can help you." He begged his father to let him rest for a while, and fell asleep curled up in a chair, with the spelling book under his head. A few minutes after he woke, his father resumed the spelling test, and to his amazement, found that his son's answers flowed freely and correctly. He went on to spell words from future lessons and even to specify which words were on which page and what illustrations went with them. This ability remained with Edgar for the rest of his life – he absorbed knowledge quite literally by sleeping on it.

Soon after the spelling test incident, Edgar suffered an accident during a games lesson at school. While playing baseball, a pitched ball hit him near the base of the spine. He seemed to be uninjured, but acted rather oddly for the rest of the day. At dinner later on that evening, he threw things at his three-year-old brother and taunted his father – things which he had never done before. When he went to bed, he began to talk in his sleep. His parents were watching over him as he slept, and his words actually formed into complete sentences, rather than the usual gibberish expected from those who talk in their sleep. It soon became apparent to his parents that Edgar was telling them that he was in shock, and to cure his condition they should make him a poultice of cornmeal, onions and herbs, and apply it to the back of his head. They duly did, and the next morning Edgar was back to normal, though he had no memory of the events. This is widely accepted as being Edgar Cayce's first psychic reading.

Edgar was a deeply religious Christian, and was unsure of whether his new-found gift was from God or the devil. For the next eleven years, because of fear of where his gift had come from, he made very little use of his psychic abilities, until the time his throat paralysis took hold of him. This affliction occurred at a time when Edgar was apprenticed to a photographer, and was hoping to earn enough money to marry his fiancée, Gertrude Evans. This was evidently not a good time to be unable to talk above a muffled rasp, and the affliction began seriously to impinge on both his career and his love life.

Cayce turned to hypnotism as a possible cure, after the medical profession had proven to be baffled by his affliction. A local hypnotist, who had heard of Edgar's poultice cure of eleven years before, proposed that he put Edgar into a trance and have him diagnose himself. Desperate for a cure, Edgar agreed to give it a go. As Edgar fell asleep, Layne suggested to him that he look inside his own body and pinpoint the trouble with his throat. Cayce began to mumble, and then to speak in a clear voice. According to his biographers, Cayce said the following:

"Yes, we can see the body. In the normal state this

> *body is unable to speak due to a partial paralysis*
> *of the inferior muscles of the vocal cords,*
> *produced by nerve strain. This is a psychological*
> *condition producing a physical effect. This may be*
> *removed by increasing the circulation to the*
> *affected parts by suggestion while in this uncon-*
> *scious condition."*

The hypnotist was truly amazed. The voice came from Edgar, but was not his – he never spoke in that manner, and was at any rate incapable of clear speech because of his throat condition. Nevertheless, the hypnotist suggested to Edgar that he increase the circulation to his throat, and watched what happened for the next twenty minutes in utter astonishment. Edgar's throat turned pink, and through various shades until it was crimson with the increased blood flow. Finally, Edgar spoke again:

> *"It is all right now. The condition is removed.*
> *Make the suggestion that the circulation return to*
> *normal, and that after that the body awaken."*

Again Layne complied, and when Edgar woke up, his voice was fully restored. Layne tried to persuade Edgar to use his amazing abilities to help others, but Edgar was reluctant to do so because of his ingrained religious fears. He also knew nothing of his unconscious pronouncements other than what he was told, and had absolutely no control over them. Finally, though, he reluctantly agreed that it was his duty to try to help others with his amazing psychic powers.

Over the next twenty-two years, Cayce did thousands of medical readings. There are nearly 20,000 of

Cayce's readings on record, and over 14,000 of these are concerned with the diagnosing of disease and the outlining of relevant treatments. Many people who came to Cayce during the early part of the twentieth century did so as a last resort, having been diagnosed as incurable by physicians from the medical profession. Cayce himself had no medical training whatsoever – all of his diagnoses and suggestions for treatment were obtained from his sleeping trances. While in such a trance, his unconscious mind seemed to tap into an endless reservoir of helpful physical information. He could, using this method, accurately diagnose illness and prescribe treatment for people he had never met or seen. Many of his "patients" never actually met him, simply writing a letter asking for his advice and in return receiving a reading which diagnosed the origin of their physical problem and recommending a course of treatment.

Cayce was an intensely private man, and the newspaper reports of his psychic powers inevitably began to flood in. He suffered a great deal from the notoriety that his work attracted, and was deeply hurt by the constant accusations of fraud which he faced. But there was worse to come. In November 1931, Cayce fell foul of the law. Two women had requested a reading from him, but they were in fact police officers, and when he accepted their request, they arrested him. He was charged under a 1927 New York statute which declared that telling fortunes for money, or with an intent to defraud, was a misdemeanour. At the hearing before a magistrate, Cayce was asked about claims that he was a psychic. His response was characteristic of his very reluctance at being a psychic:

"I make no claims whatsoever. For thirty-one years I have been told I was a psychic. It first began as a child. I didn't know what it was. After it had gone on for years, a company was formed to study my work."

That company is still in existence today, and continues to investigate Cayce's legacy. The company was set up in 1931 to study and preserve Cayce's work, and is called the Association of Research and Enlightenment (ARE). The magistrate presiding over Edgar's case decided that the ARE was "an incorporated ecclesiastical body", and threw the case out of court. He told the police that they had no right to tamper with the beliefs of an ecclesiastical body, and besides, he believed that Cayce had never intended to commit any fraud. But the case had a very negative effect on Cayce, despite the fact that it had a favourable outcome. He fell into a depression, and began to wonder if his apparent psychic gifts were of any use, and considered giving up his healing work. He had always longed for people to believe in his ability, and had at an early stage in his "career" submitted himself to testing by scientists.

In 1906, he let a friend of his, who was a physician, persuade him to perform a reading in front of an audience which contained a host of doctors. Once Cayce had fallen into his sleep trance, a debate arose in the audience about the nature of his so-called powers. Some argued that he was under self-hypnosis, others that he was receiving dream messages while in a trance, and yet others that he was quite simply a faker. One of the doctors rose from the audience and stuck a needle in Edgar's arms, hands and feet to see how he would react. When there was no response, another member of the audience pushed a hatpin all the way through Edgar's cheek. Another sceptic in the audience went even further, and took out a penknife and cut off the nail from Edgar's left forefinger, and there was still no indication of either pain or blood. But when Cayce awoke, he was, naturally, in agony, and lost his temper. He declared that he would "never try to prove anything to any one of you again".

Despite the scepticism of the medical profession, people who had come to Cayce for help reported remarkable cures, and were more than happy to pay for them. Cayce, however, was against taking money in return for his services, even though he was on the brink of bankruptcy several times throughout his life. Only when he was absolutely desperate would he accept money for his gift, until he finally decided to give up his other career as a photographer and devote his full attention to his psychic readings. Even when he had chosen to use his abilities as his career, he never turned anyone away because they lacked the money to pay for his services.

In the very year that he chose to become a full-time psychic, Cayce was contacted by Arthur Lammers, who was to prove a catalyst in changing Cayce's life. Lammers, as so many had done before him, sought out Cayce for some readings, but this time not for healing purposes. He asked Cayce about such things as astrology, the workings of the subconscious and the nature of the soul. Cayce initially agreed to give Lammers a reading on astrology, but the end result of the reading was to confirm the reality of reincarnation. While in the sleep trance, Cayce told Lammers that humans did indeed experience successive life-times for the purpose of perfecting their souls, the ultimate aim being the union of these souls with God. This meeting with Lammers led Cayce to perform new readings, which he called "life readings". He would start with the astrological conditions of the subject's birth, and then the life reading would turn to several of the person's past incarnations. The aim of these readings was to find information from past lives that could make the present incarnation happier. In his normal state, Cayce was unable to explain how he was able to perform such amazing readings. However, he did once offer an explanation while in a sleep trance:

> "Edgar Cayce's mind is amenable to suggestion, the same as all other subconscious minds, but in addition thereto it has the power to interpret to the objective mind of others what it acquires from the subconscious mind of other individuals of the same kind. The subconscious mind forgets nothing. The conscious mind receives the impression from without and transfers all thought to the subconscious, where it remains even though the conscious be destroyed."

Many theorists have declared that Cayce was simply a clairvoyant whose abilities allowed him to see into people's bodies at a distance to diagnose ailments, as well as to see into the past and the future. Cayce himself thought that he was simply accessing the knowledge of some transcendental mind, what Carl Jung would call the collective unconscious. Cayce described this mind pool as God's book of remembrance or the universal consciousness. He also came up with the term "Akashic records", which many now believe hold the knowledge of humanity from the beginning of time.

In one of his readings, Cayce came up with a description of the Akashic records:

> *"Upon time and space is written the thoughts, the deeds, the activities of an entity – as in relationships to its environs, its hereditary influence; as directed – or judgment drawn by or according to what the entity's ideal is. Hence it has been oft called, the record is God's book of remembrance; and each entity, each soul – as the activities of a single day of an entity in the material world – either makes some good or bad or indifferent [effect], depending upon the entity's application of self towards that which is the ideal manner for the use of time, opportunity and expression of that for which each soul enters a material manifestation. The interpretation then as drawn here is with the desire and hope that, in opening this for the entity, the experience may be one of helpfulness and hopefulness."*

Cayce's readings became ever more strange. He had started off with simple healing, but eventually moved on to prophecy and tales of human history. The most famous of these tales concerned the mythical civilization of Atlantis. According to Cayce, Atlantis was one of the most advanced civilizations that the world has ever known and will ever know. Much of modern technology is simply the rediscovery of knowledge and information possessed by the

Atlantean culture. Apparently, the Atlanteans lost their sense of purpose by becoming too attached to power and the material world. In time, this once spiritual populace became fractured and split into two distinct groups: the Children of the Law of One; and the Sons of Belial. Those of the former group carried on the spiritual tradition of their forefathers, while those of the latter group became engrossed with satisfying their physical appetites and desires. This split would eventually lead to the continent's downfall and eventual destruction. By focusing upon materiality and ignoring their true spiritual nature, the people of Atlantis brought upon themselves a series of three cataclysms. The first, about 50,000 BC, destroyed a major power source. The second, about 28,500 BC, caused the continent to split into three smaller islands: Poseidia, Og and Aryan. The third and final disaster occurred around 10,500 BC, and caused the three islands to sink, forcing those few who survived to migrate to other parts of the world. Cayce alleged that, prior to the final destruction of Atlantis, many of the people migrated to Egypt and were absorbed into a culture that reached its height of glory at about the same time as the third Atlantean cataclysm. Cayce stated that records of the once glorious civilization of Atlantis would be found in Egypt.

Cayce also claimed to have been through a number of previous incarnations, which included a warrior during the Trojan wars, a disciple of Jesus Christ, an Egyptian priest, a Persian monarch and a heavenly angel-like being that had been on Earth prior to Adam and Eve. Some say that he might have lost the plot a bit, but there are still followers all over the world who firmly believe every word of his readings. The prophecies that came through in Cayce's readings were largely unsuccessful. In 1934, he declared that Poseidia (one of the islands of Atlantis) would be the first part of the ancient continent to rise again from the Atlantic ocean. He prophesied that this would happen in 1968 or 1969. This clearly did not happen. As is so often the case with prophets, he also predicted disasters of biblical proportions. One of his readings foretold of great changes to the Earth, and many of his followers had a forty-year time window in which to hold their breath, awaiting the prophesied doom:

> *"The earth will be broken up in the western portion of America. The greater portion of Japan must go into the sea. The upper portion of Europe will be changed as in the twinkling of an eye. Land will appear off the east coast of America. There will be the upheavals in the Arctic and the Antarctic that will make for the eruption of volcanoes in the Torrid areas, and there will be the shifting then of the poles – so that where there have been those of a frigid or semi-tropical [climate] will become the more tropical, and moss and fern will grow. And these will begin in those periods in '58 and '98."*

Perhaps Cayce should have stuck to the healing. None of the above happened, and yet the society which Cayce founded, the ARE, still maintains that he was correct! All that the society has done is to reinterpret what Cayce said, claiming that what he prophesied did not really mean the end of the world as we know it, but was the dawning of a New Age of hope for all humankind. All you have to do to be a part of this great new global community is to devote your life to reading Cayce's work, and join the ARE. I would advise caution before following this path.

Bibliography

Bernstein, Morey, *The Search for Bridie Murphy*, Bantam, 1990

Blackmore, Susan, *Dying to Live*, Grafton, 1993

Calkins, Carroll C. (ed.), *Mysteries of the Unknown*, The Reader's Digest Association, 1982

Carrington, Hereward, *The Story of Psychic Science*, Rider, 1930

Cheetham, Erika, *The Prophecies of Nostradamus*, Peerage Books, 1989

Chopra, Deepak, MD, *Quantum Healing*, Bantam, 1989

Crichton, Michael, *Travels*, Pan Books, 1988

Davis, Stephen, *Future Sex*, Globe Press Pty Ltd, 1991

De Liso, Oscar, *Padre Pio, the Priest Who Bears the Wounds of Christ*, McGraw Hill, 1960

Ebon, Martin, *Prophecy in Our Time*, The New American Library, 1968

Ellis, Keith, *Prediction and Prophecy*, Wayland Publishers, 1973

Fenimore, Angie, *Beyond Darkness: My Near-Death Journey to Hell and Back*, Simon and Schuster, 1995

Frank, Gerald, *The Boston Strangler*, Handbooks Ltd, 1996

Gregory, Richard L. (ed.), *The Oxford Companion to the Mind*, Oxford University Press, 1987

Gurney, Edmund, et al, *Phantasms of the Living*, Trübner and Company, 1886

Gurney, Edmund, Myers, Frederick W. H., & Podmore, Frank, *Phantasms of the Living*, Kegan, Paul, Trench, Trubner & Co, 1918

Hamilton-Parker, Craig, *The Psychic Casebook*, Cassell, 1999

Harrison, Michael, *Fire From Heaven: A Study of Spontaneous Combustion in Human Beings*, Methuen, 1976

Harrison, Ted, *Stigmata*, HarperCollins, 1994

Hicks, Jim (ed.), *Psychic Powers*, Time Life Books, 1991

Hicks, Jim (ed.), *Psychic Voyages*, Time Life Books, 1991

Hicks, Jim (ed.), *Spirit Summonings*, Time Life Books, 1991

Hicks, Jim (ed.), *The Mind and Beyond*, Time Life Books, 1991

Jung, Carl G. & Pauli, W., *The Interpretation of Nature and the Psyche*, Pantheon Books, 1955

Jung, Carl G., *Synchronicity: An Acausal Connecting Principle*, Bollingen Foundation, 1960

Kalweit, Holger, *Shamans, Healers and Medicine Men*, Shambala, 1992

King, Francis X., *The Encyclopedia of Magic, Mind & Mysteries*, Dorling Kindersley, 1991

Margolis, Jonathan, *Uri Geller Magician or Mystic?*, Orion, 1998

Métraux, Alfred, *Voodoo in Haiti*, Sphere Books Ltd, 1974

Moody, J. R. M. D., Raymond, A., *Life After Life*, Phantom Books, 1976

Ostrander, Sheila & Schroeder, Lynn, *Psychic Discoveries: The Iron Curtain Lifted*, Souvenir Press, 1980

Randi, James, *An Encyclopedia of Claims, Frauds and Hoaxes of the Occult and Supernatural*, St Martin's Griffin, 1997

Randles, Jenny, *Paranormal Source Book*, Piatkus, 1999

Rhine, J. B., *The Reach of the Mind*, William Sloane Associates Inc., 1947

Ring, Kenneth, *The Omega Project*, William Morrow, 1992

Rogo, D. Scott, *Life After Death*, Geld Publishing, 1986

Rogo, D. Scott, *The Poltergeist Experience*, Penguin Books, 1979

Roll, William G., et al, *Research in Parapsychology*, The Scarecrow Press Inc, 1973

Sagan, Carl, *The Cosmic Connection: An Extra-terrestrial Perspective*, Anchor Press, 1973

Schnabel, Jim, *Remote Viewers: The Secret History of America's Psychic Spies*, Dell Publishing, 1997

Solomon, Grant, *Psychic Surgeon*, Thorsons, 1997

Spencer, John & Spencer, Anne, *Powers of the Mind*, Orion Books Ltd, 1998

Stevenson, Ian, MD, *Twenty Cases Suggestive of Reincarnation*, The University Press of Virginia, 1974

Thurston, Herbert, *The Physical Phenomena of Mysticism*, Henry Regnery Company, 1952

Treffert, Darrold A., *Extraordinary People*, Black Swan, 1990

Wilson, Colin, *Enigmas and Mysteries*, Aldus Books Ltd, 1976

Wilson, Colin, *The Psychic Detectives*, Pan Books, 1984

A great new series of six volumes on the UnXplained. Essential reading for all fans of curious facts and strange phenomena.

MIND'S SECRETS
Discover the secrets of the Mind

Explore the most complicated and mysterious phenomenon of all: the human mind.

Mysteries investigated in this volume:

- Hidden Powers of the Mind
- Mystical and Forbidden Knowledge
- Reincarnation
- Mysteries of the Human Body
- Fate, Destiny and Coincidence
- Unknown Forces
- Jinxes and Curses
- Shadows of Death

STRANGE PEOPLE
Discover the private worlds of People

Find out about the inner thoughts and beliefs of some of the World's strangest people.

Mysteries investigated in this volume:

- Vanishings
- A World of Luck
- Hoaxes and Deceptions
- Crimes and Punishments
- Odd and Eccentric People
- All the Rage
- Manias and Delusions

VISIONARIES AND MYSTICS

Discover the secrets of Visionaries and Mystics

For centuries visionaries have explored the hidden pathways of fate. Learn about their discoveries.

Mysteries investigated in this volume:

- Mystic Places
- Visions and Prophecies
- Mystic Quests
- The Mystic Year
- Eastern Mysteries
- Search for the Soul
- Utopian Visions

STRANGE ENCOUNTERS

Discover the world of the UnXplained

Find out the truth behind the strangest phenomena ever witnessed.

Mysteries investigated in this volume:

- UFO Phenomena
- Mysterious Creatures
- Mysterious Lands and Peoples
- Alien Encounters
- Time and Space
- Hauntings
- Phantom Encounters

DREAMS AND MAGIC
Discover the secret world of Dreams and Magic
Find out about the power of dreams and magic.
Mysteries investigated in this volume:

- Ancient Wisdom and Secret Sects
- Powers of Healing
- Dreams and Dreaming
- Witches and Witchcraft
- Magical Arts
- Earth Energies
- Transformations

PSYCHIC POWERS
Discover the world of the Psychic
Find out about the inner recesses of the mind and the power of the psychic.
Mysteries investigated in this volume:

- Psychic Powers
- Psychic Voyages
- Cosmic Connections
- Spirit Summonings
- The Mind and Beyond
- Search for Immortality
- Psychics
- Mind over Matter